Thank you for choosing us!

We hope that you enjoy this coloring book! As a bonus, we included 2 additional test pages for you to mark up with your materials.

We recommend using crayons or colored pencils for this book, but if you are using markers, we suggest placing a piece of paper behind the artwork so that the ink doesn't leak through.

Again, thank you for choosing us and we appreciate your support!

Clarence Mayo | Visual Artist

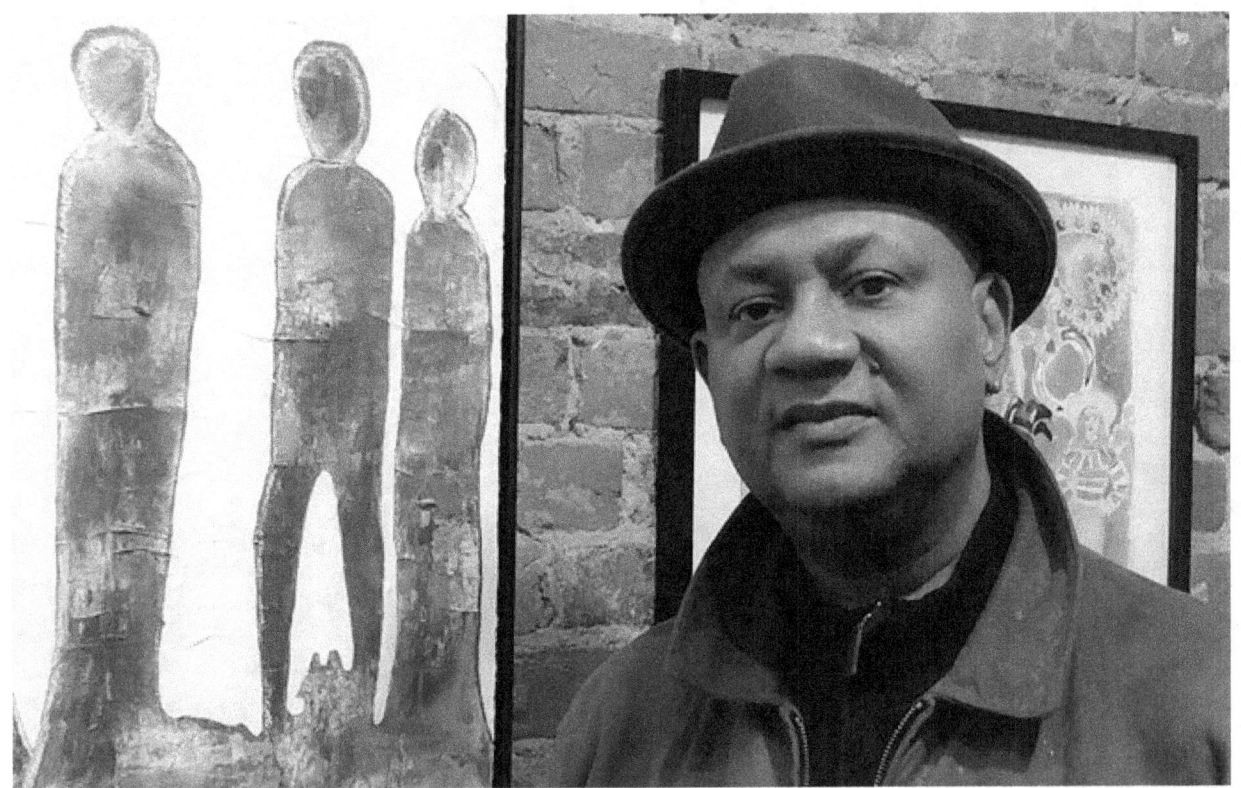

CLARENCE MAYO

About the Artist

Clarence Mayo is a local artist from Hillsborough, North Carolina. Mayo specializes in cold wax, oil, & acrylic. Mayo's work is inspired by tribal icons & symbols from various cultures around the world. He is particularly inspired by African and Central American art and culture.

This coloring book contains his recent series of abstract tribal sketchbook drawings. His drawings are created using the "automatic drawing" method allowing the pencil to move randomly and freely across the paper or other surfaces. Each mark is made using this method and is later filled in with random figures, colors, lines, or patterns.

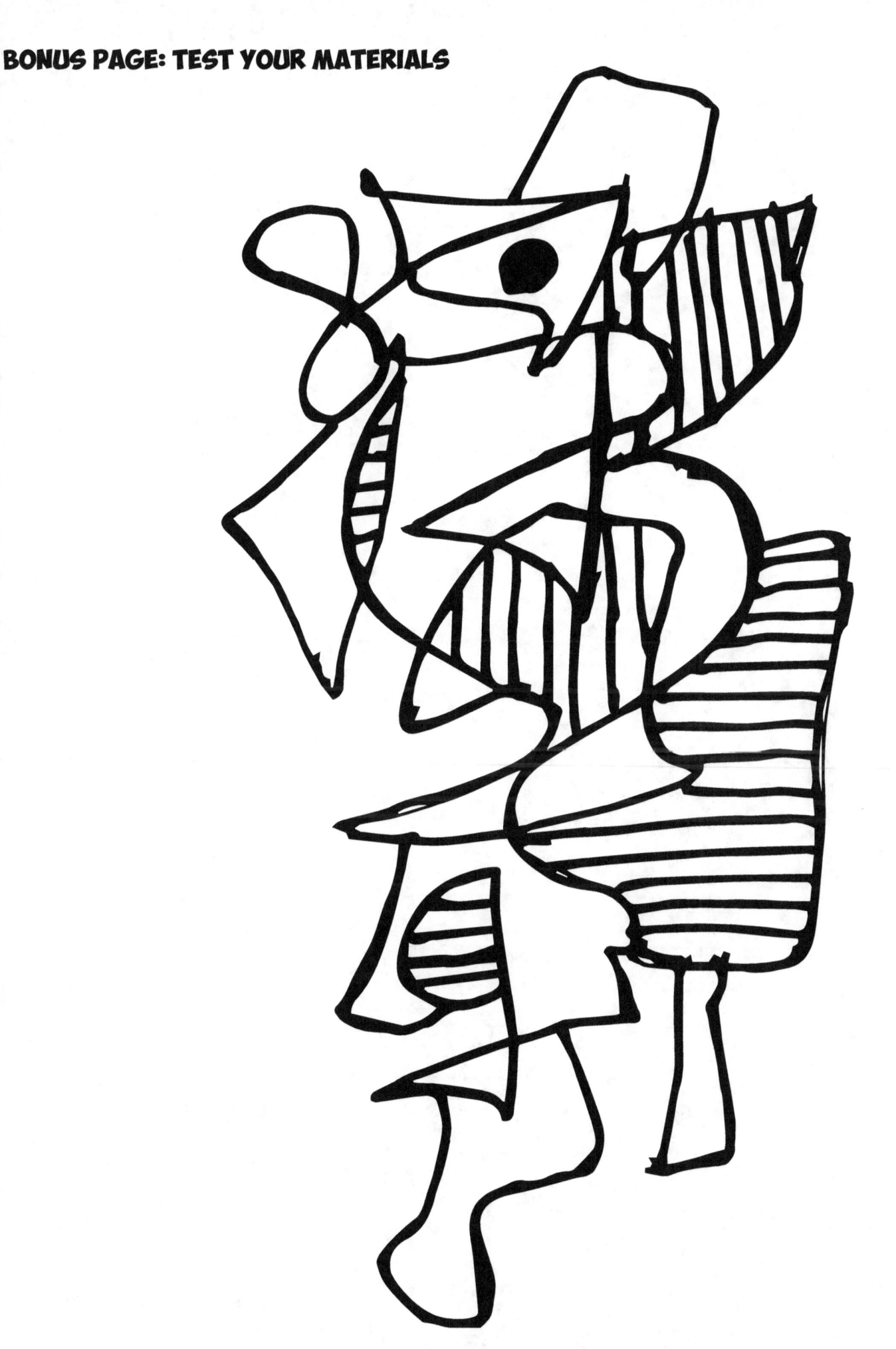

BONUS PAGE: TEST YOUR MATERIALS

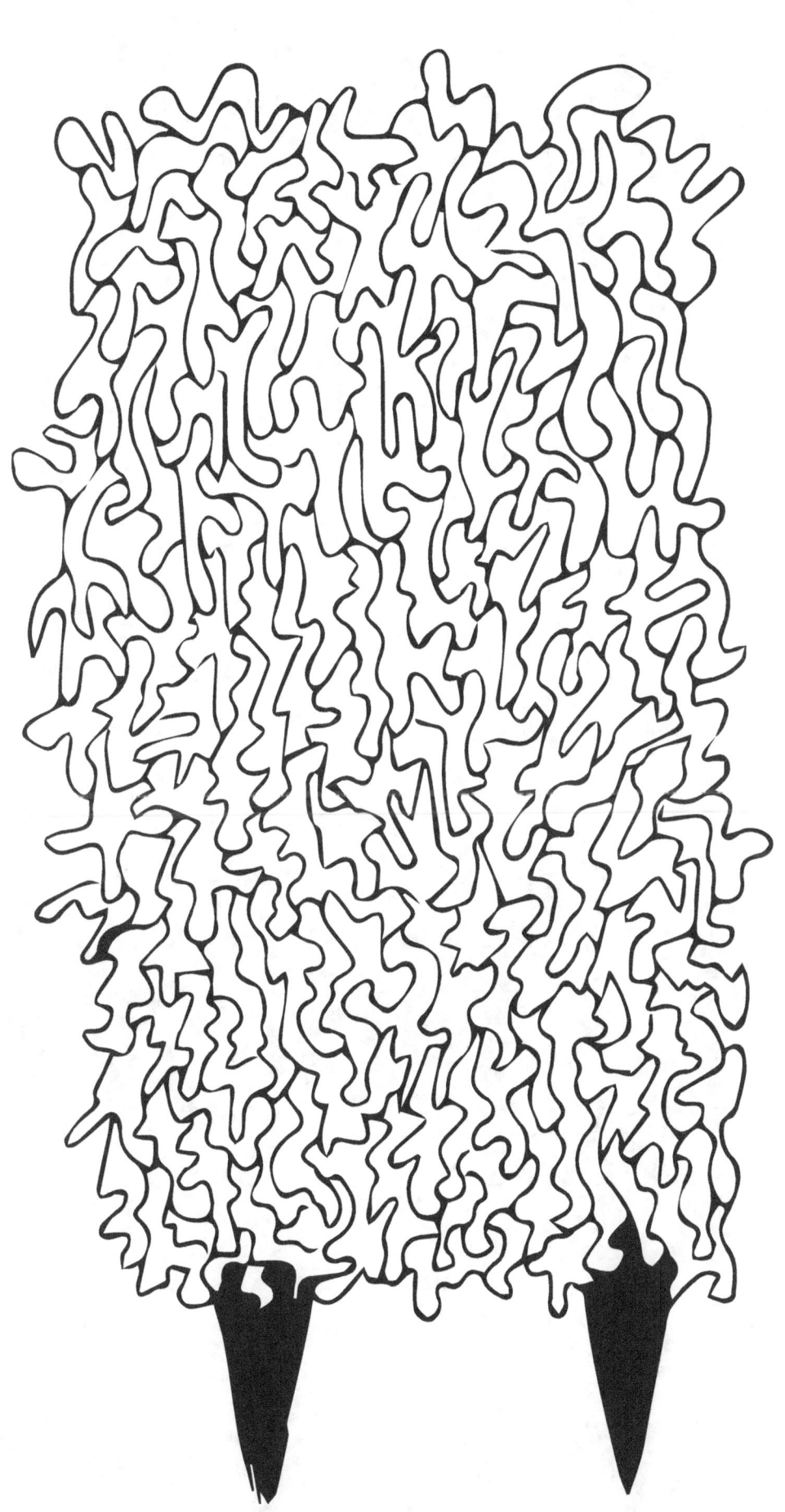

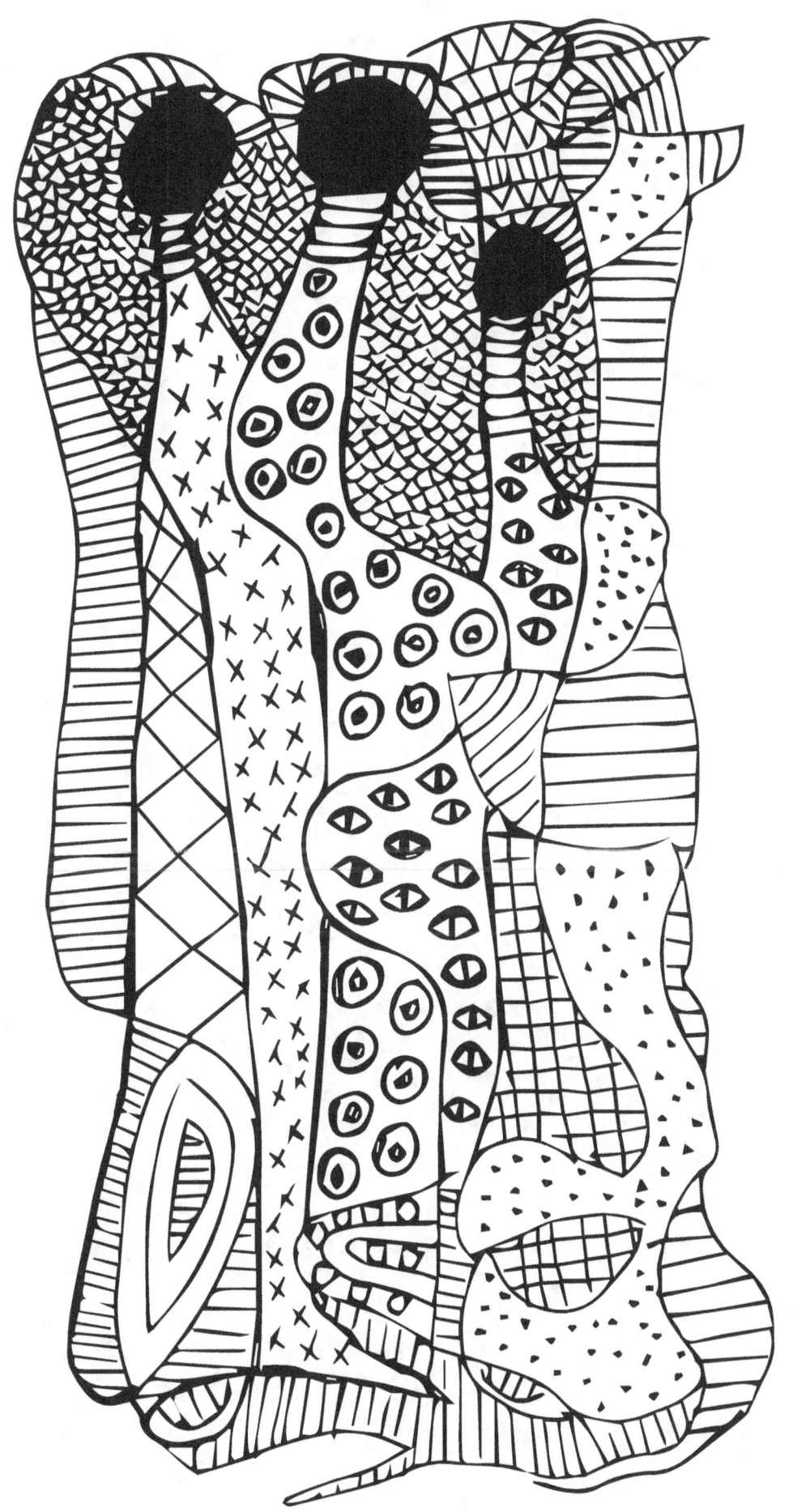

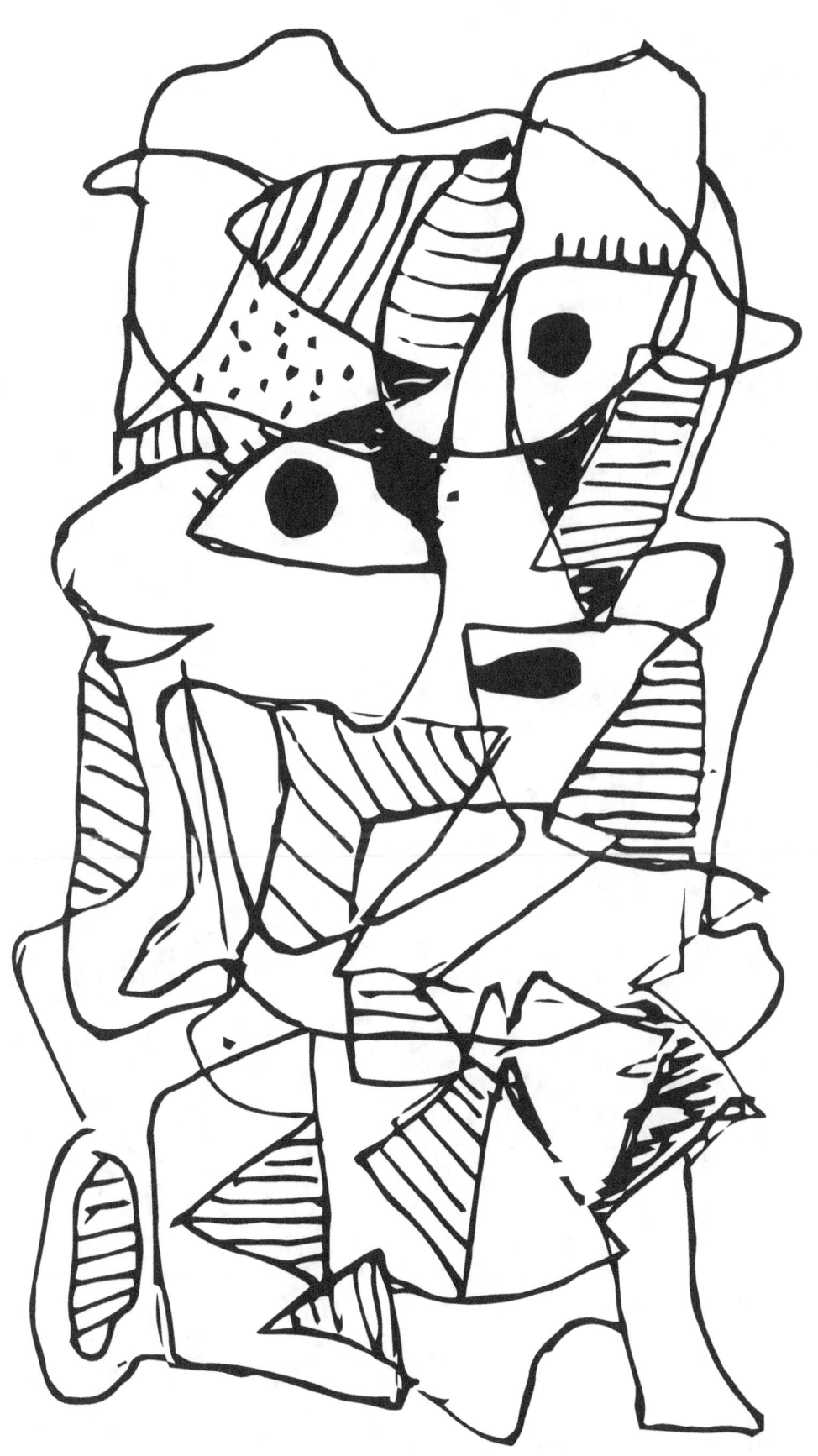

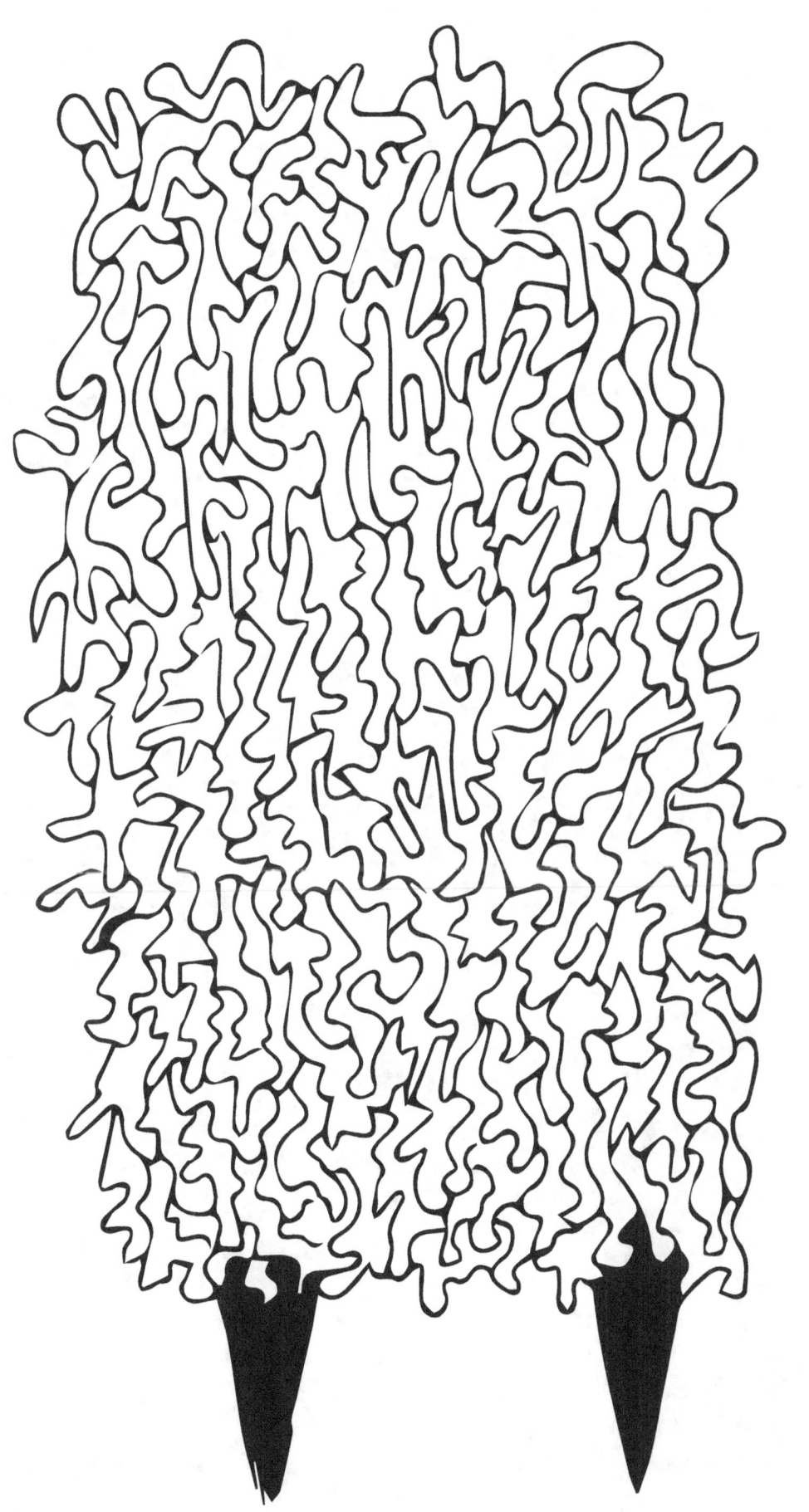

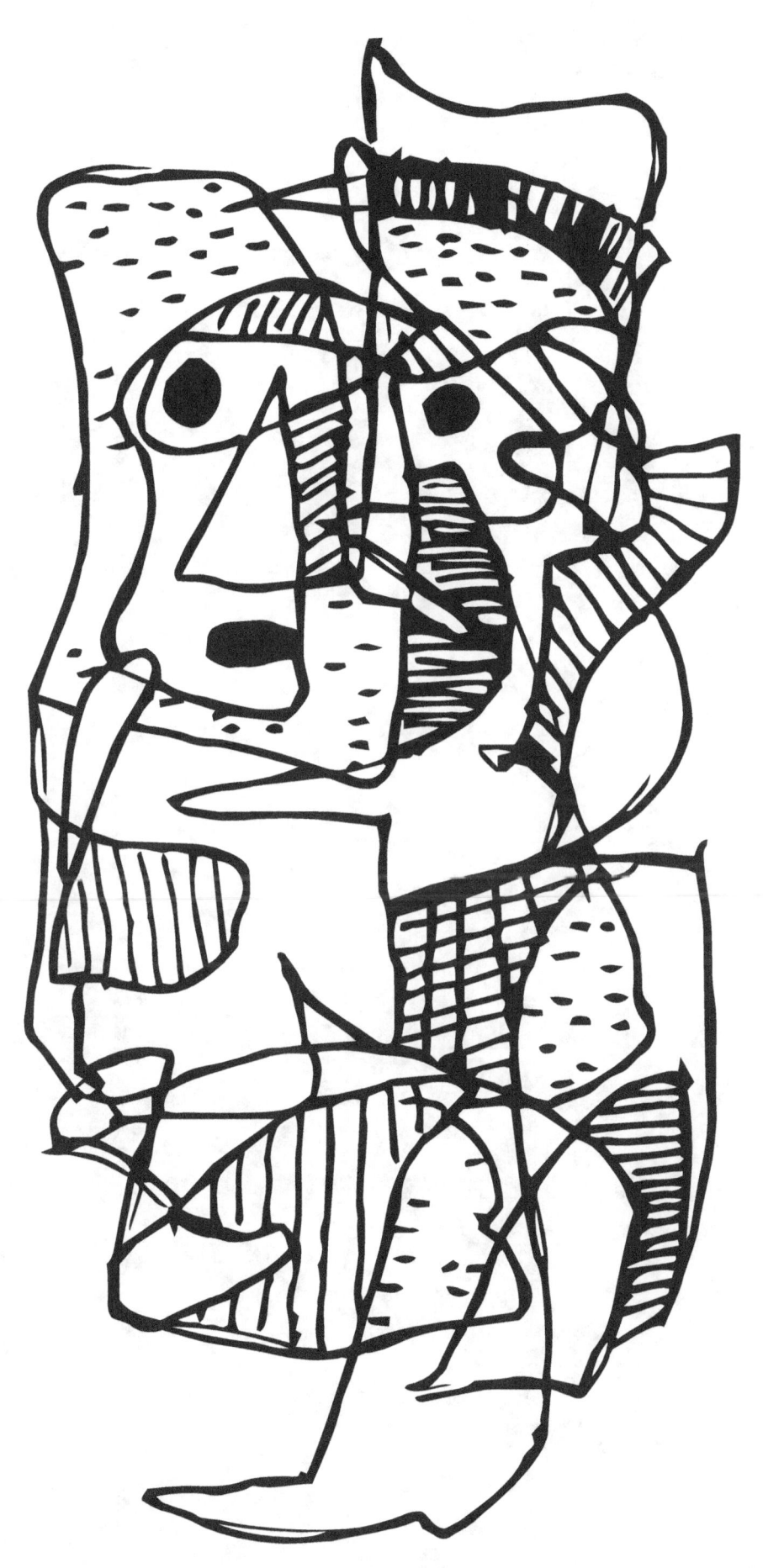

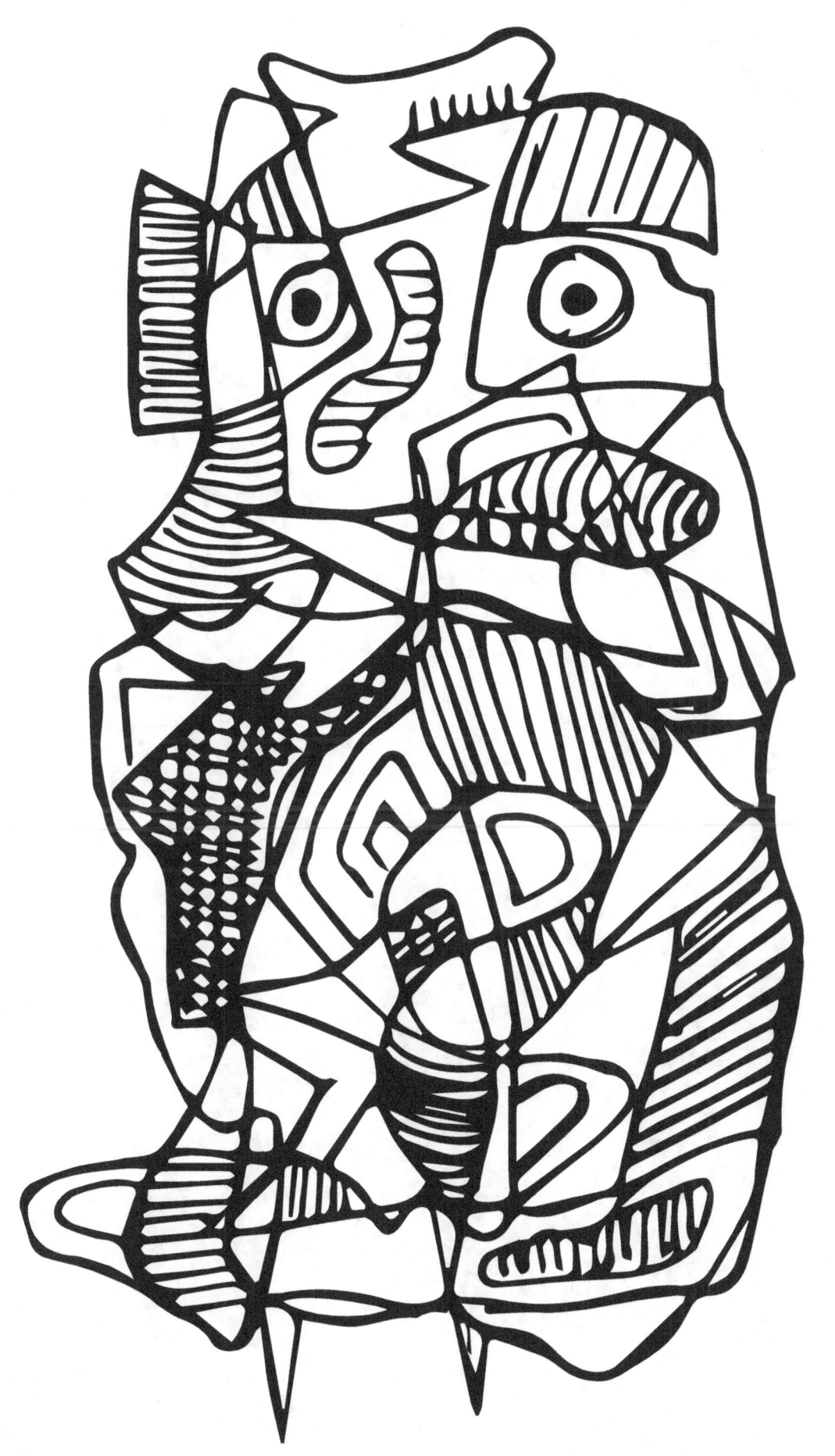

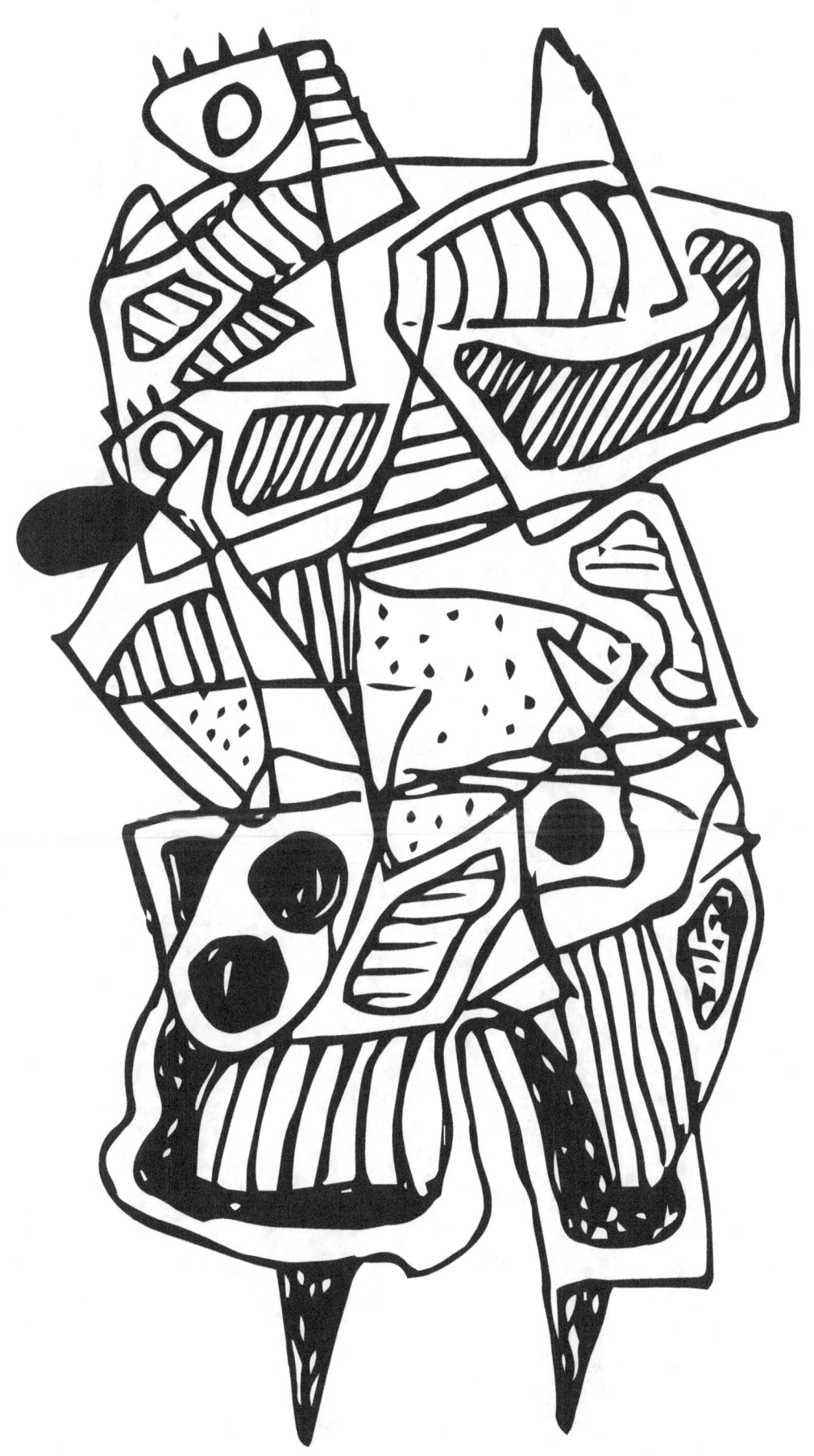

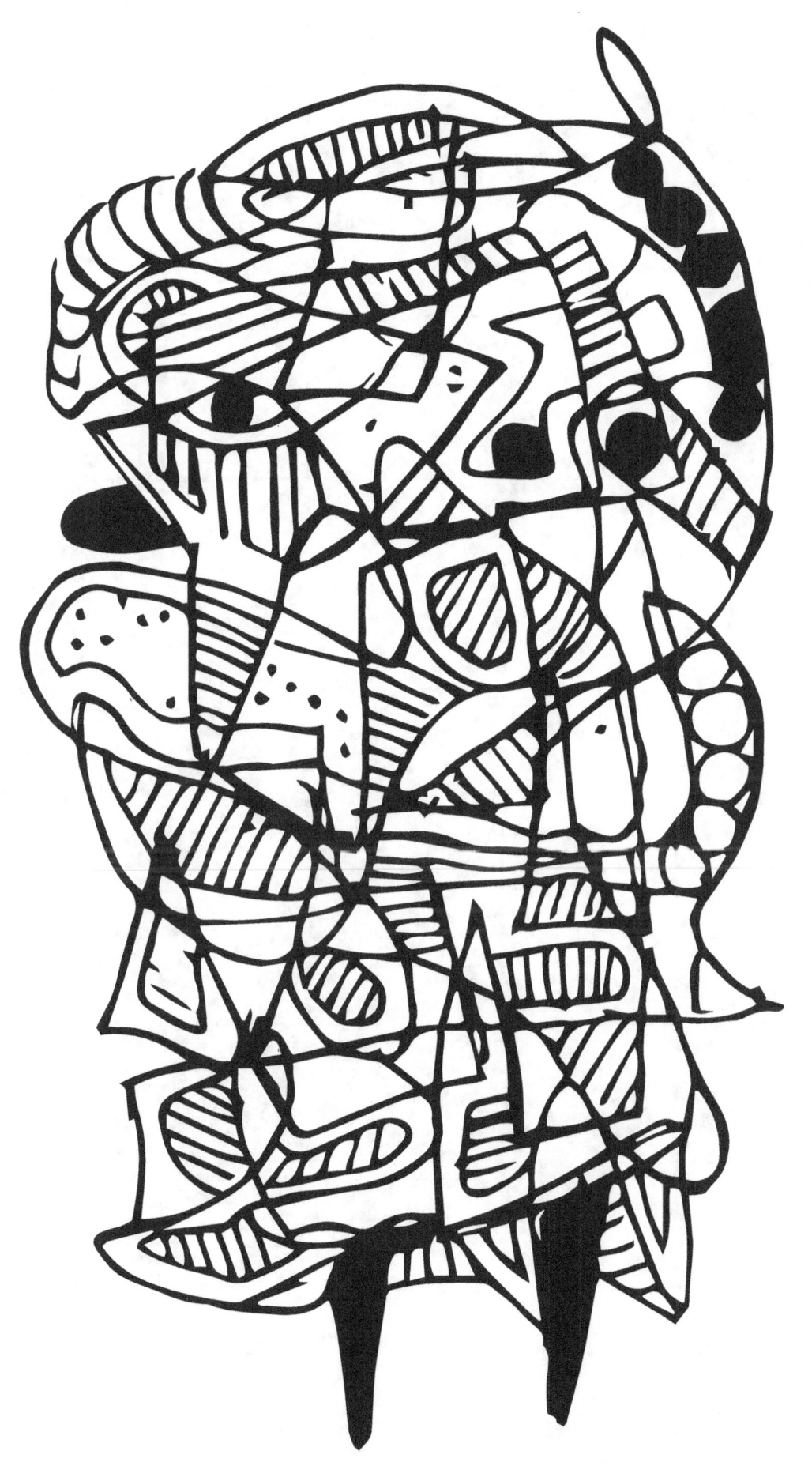

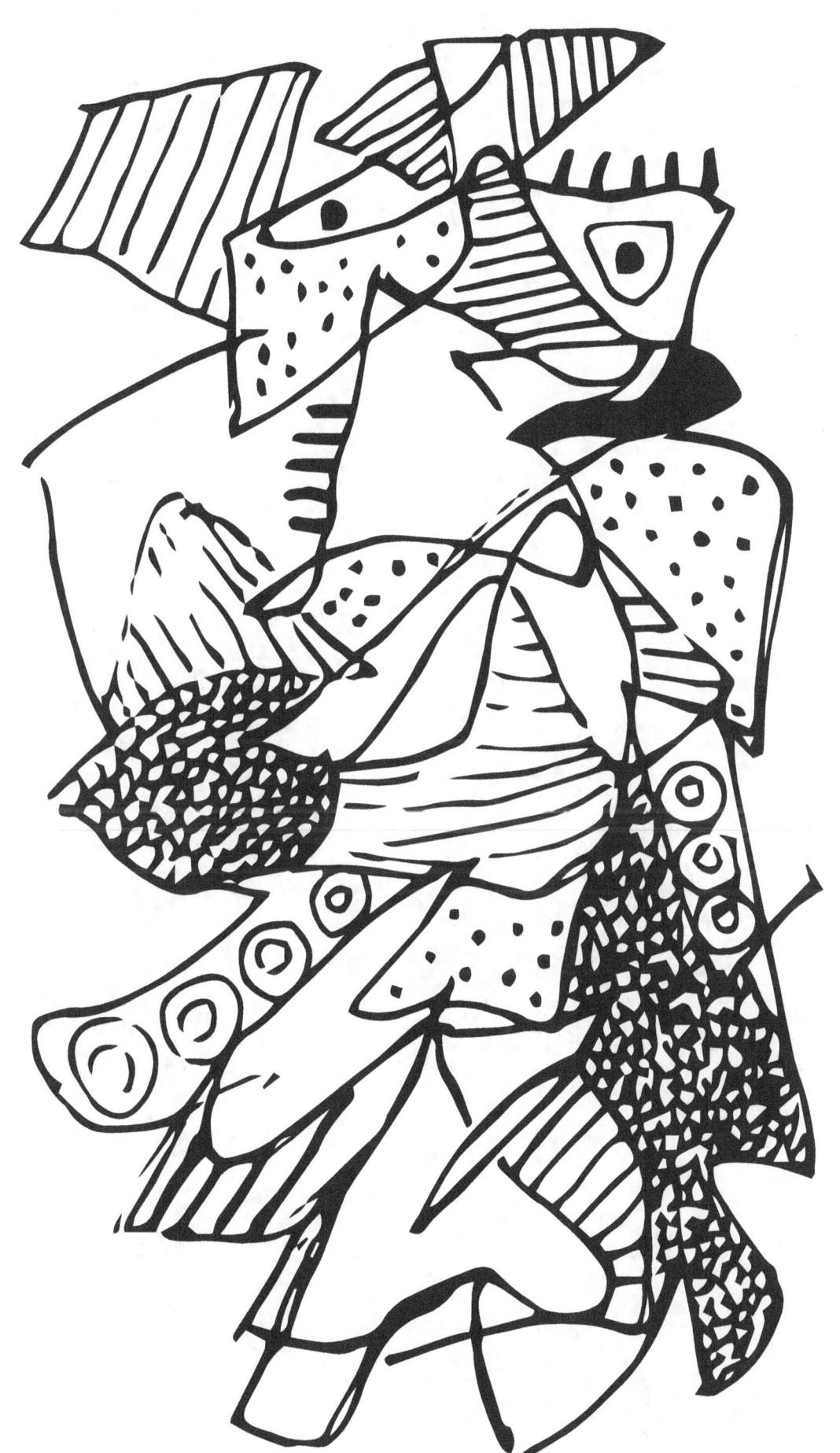

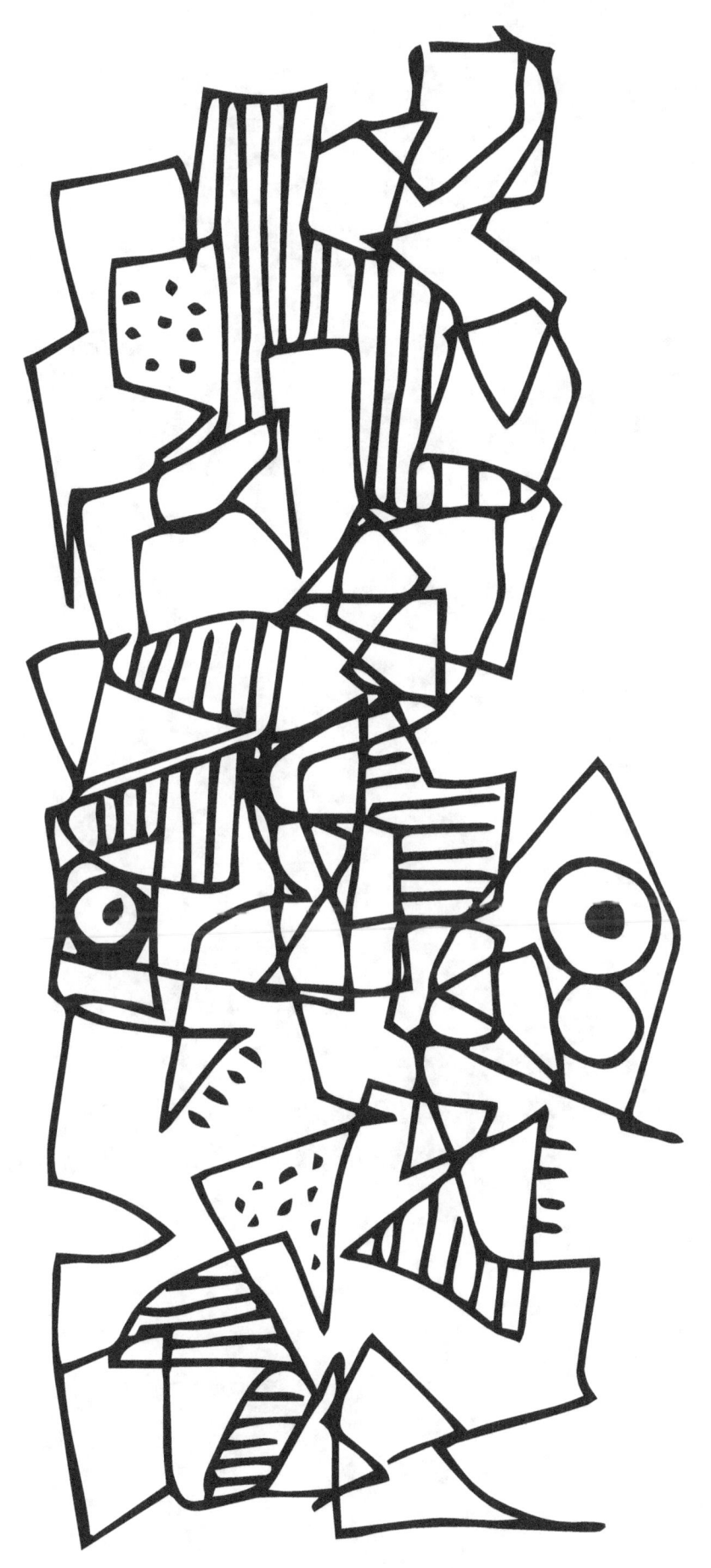

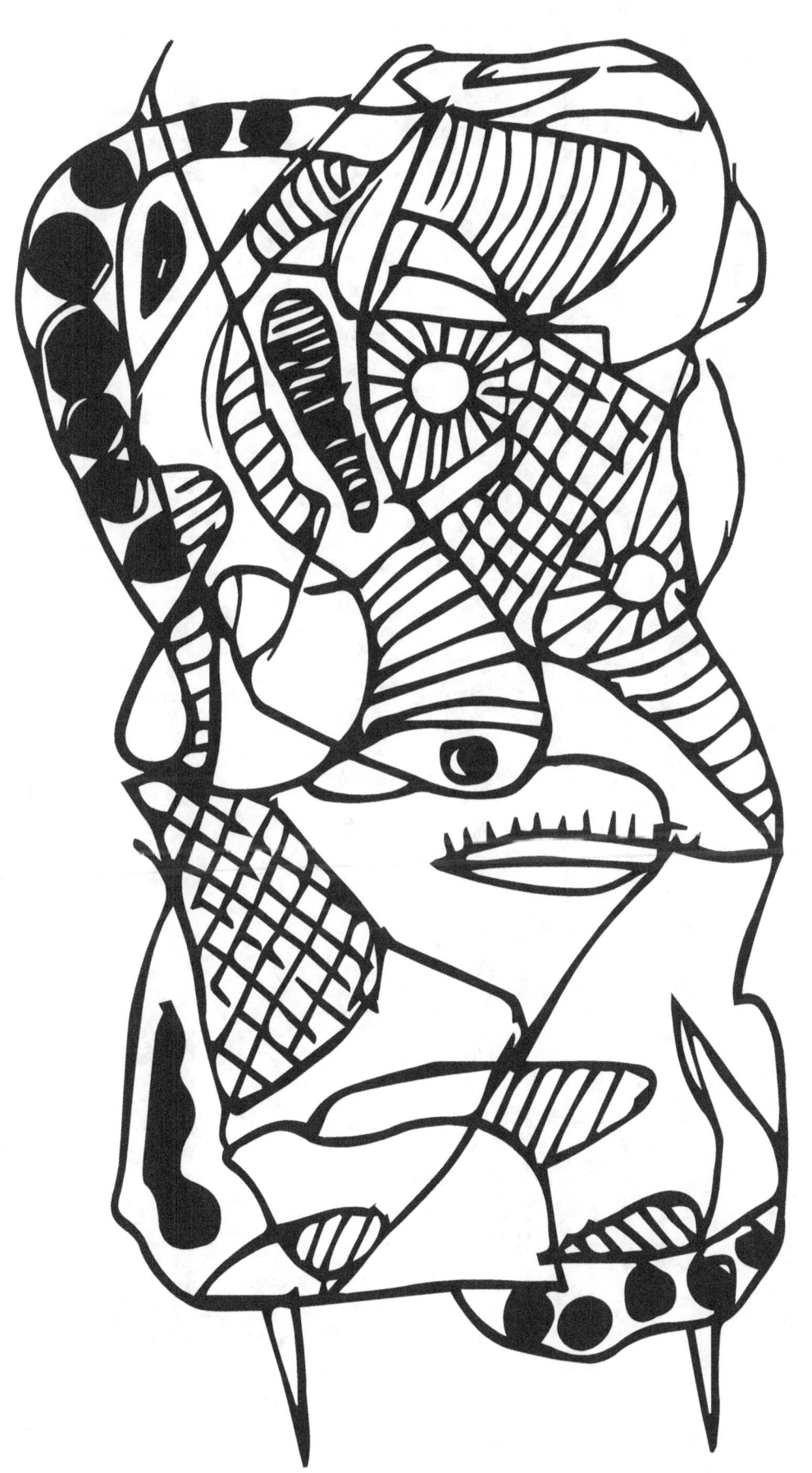

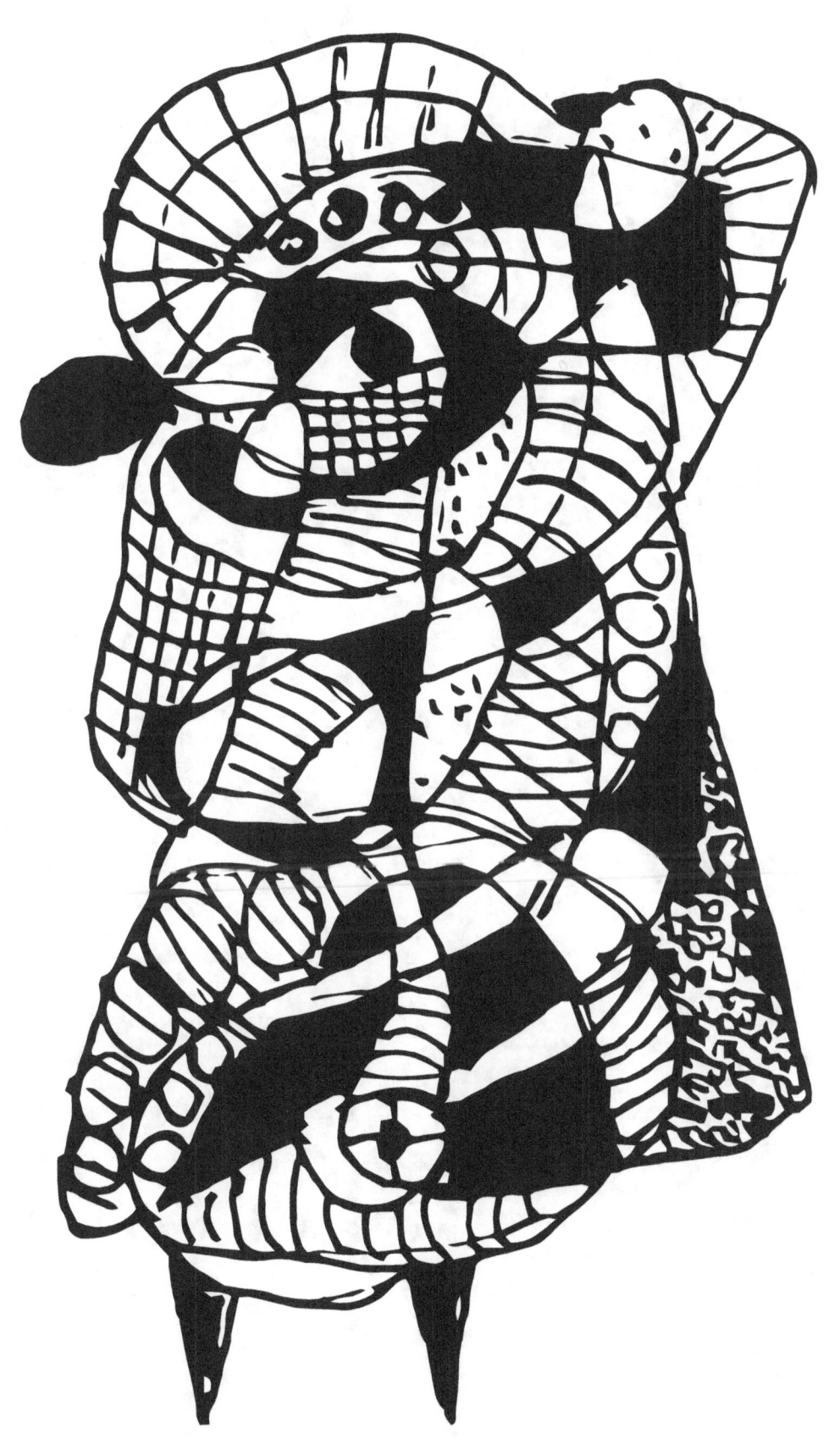

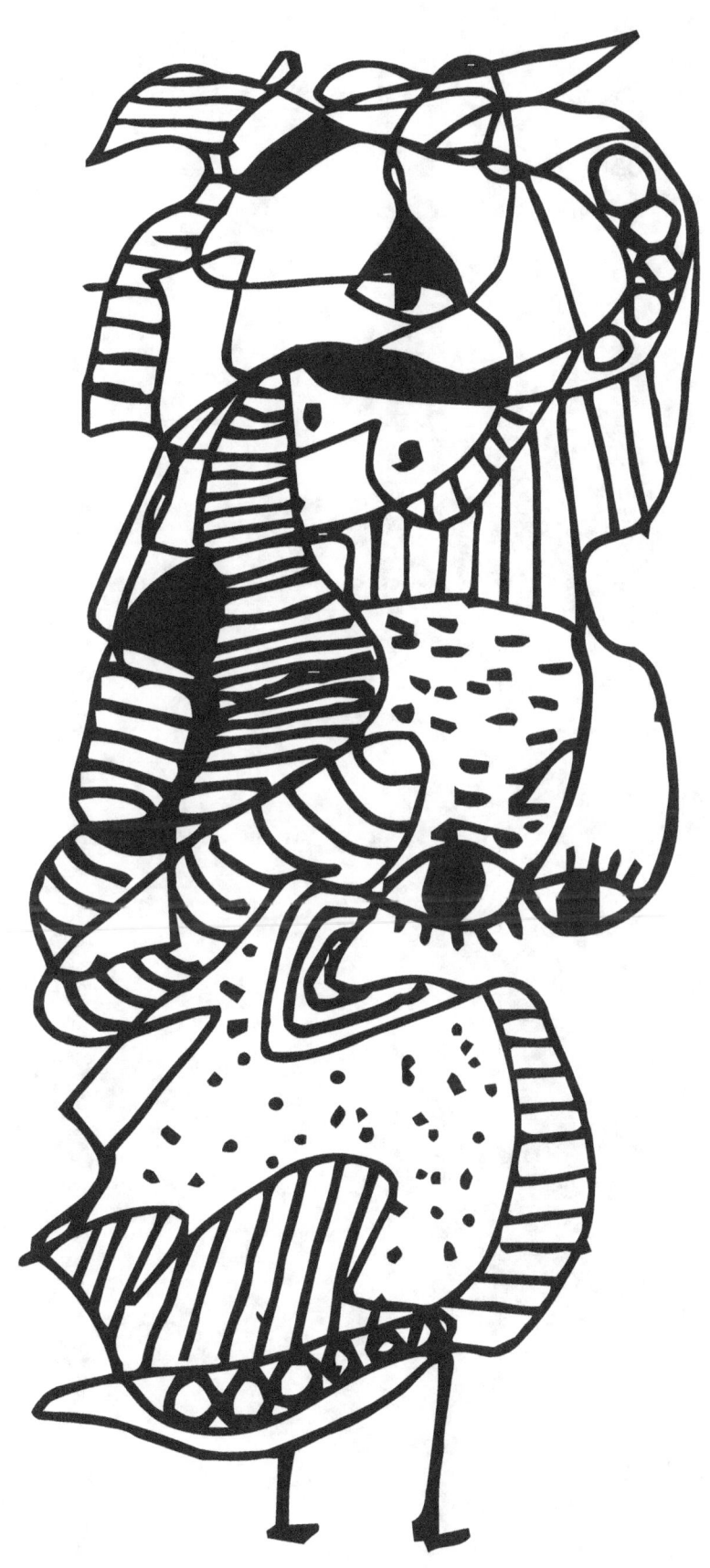

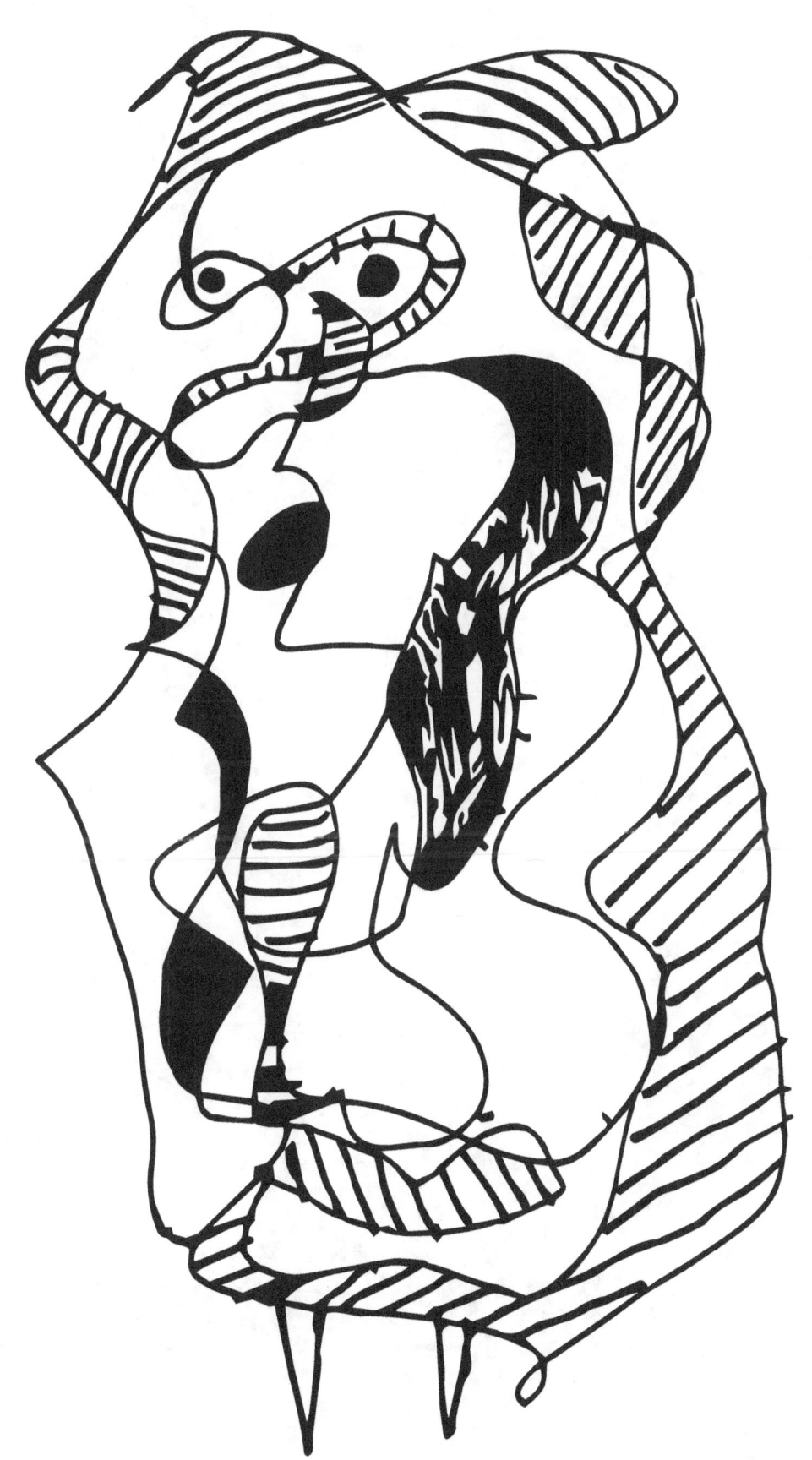

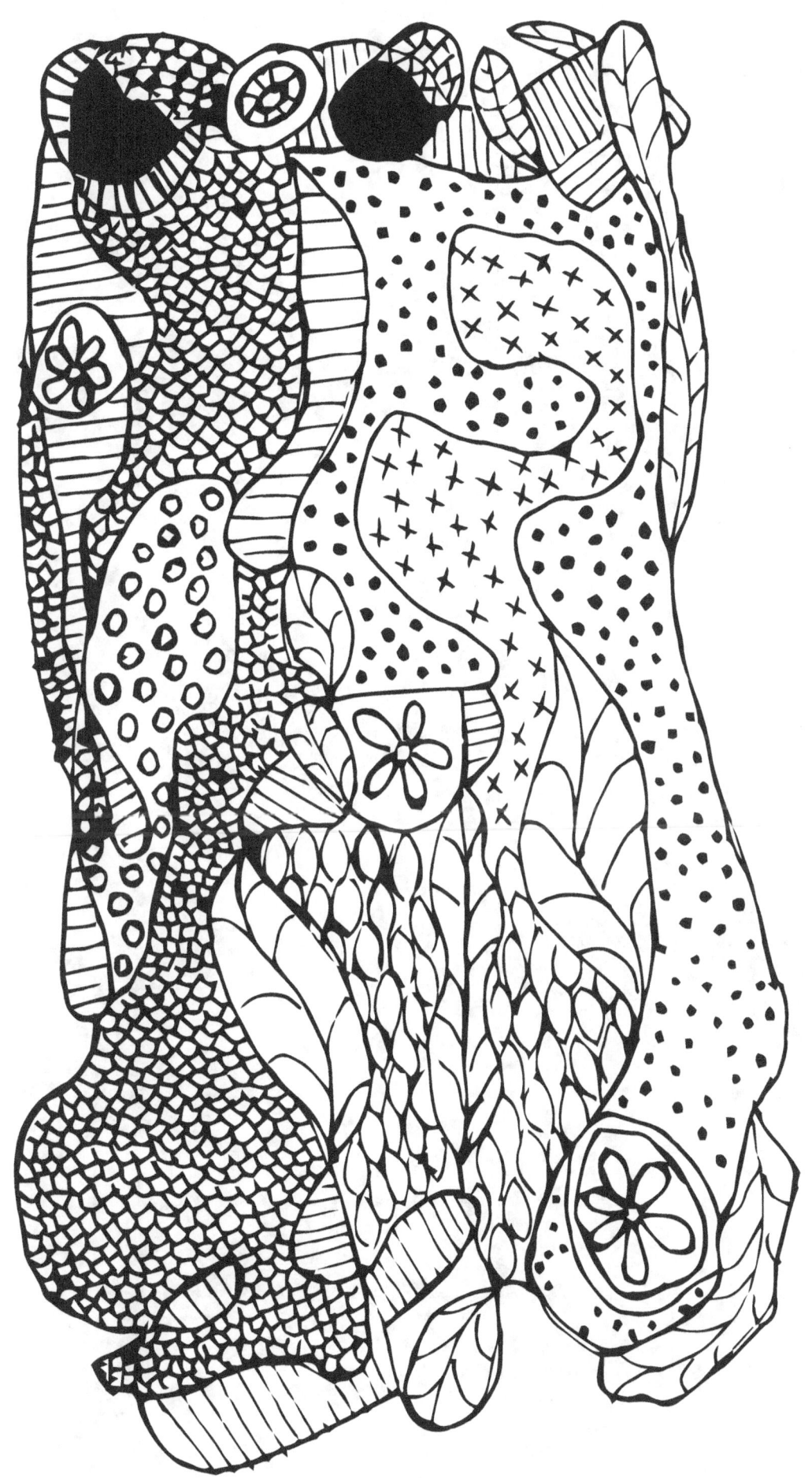

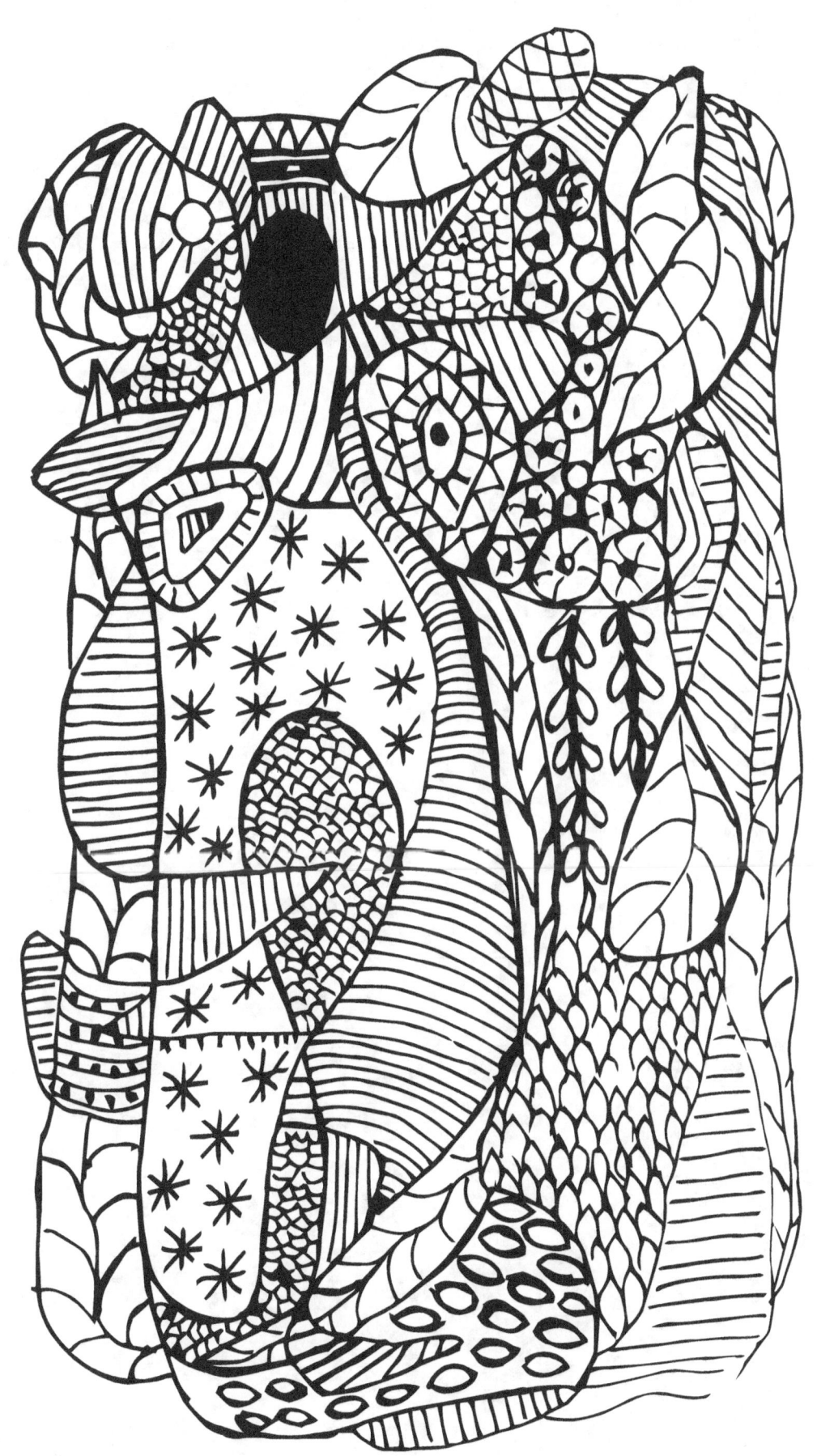

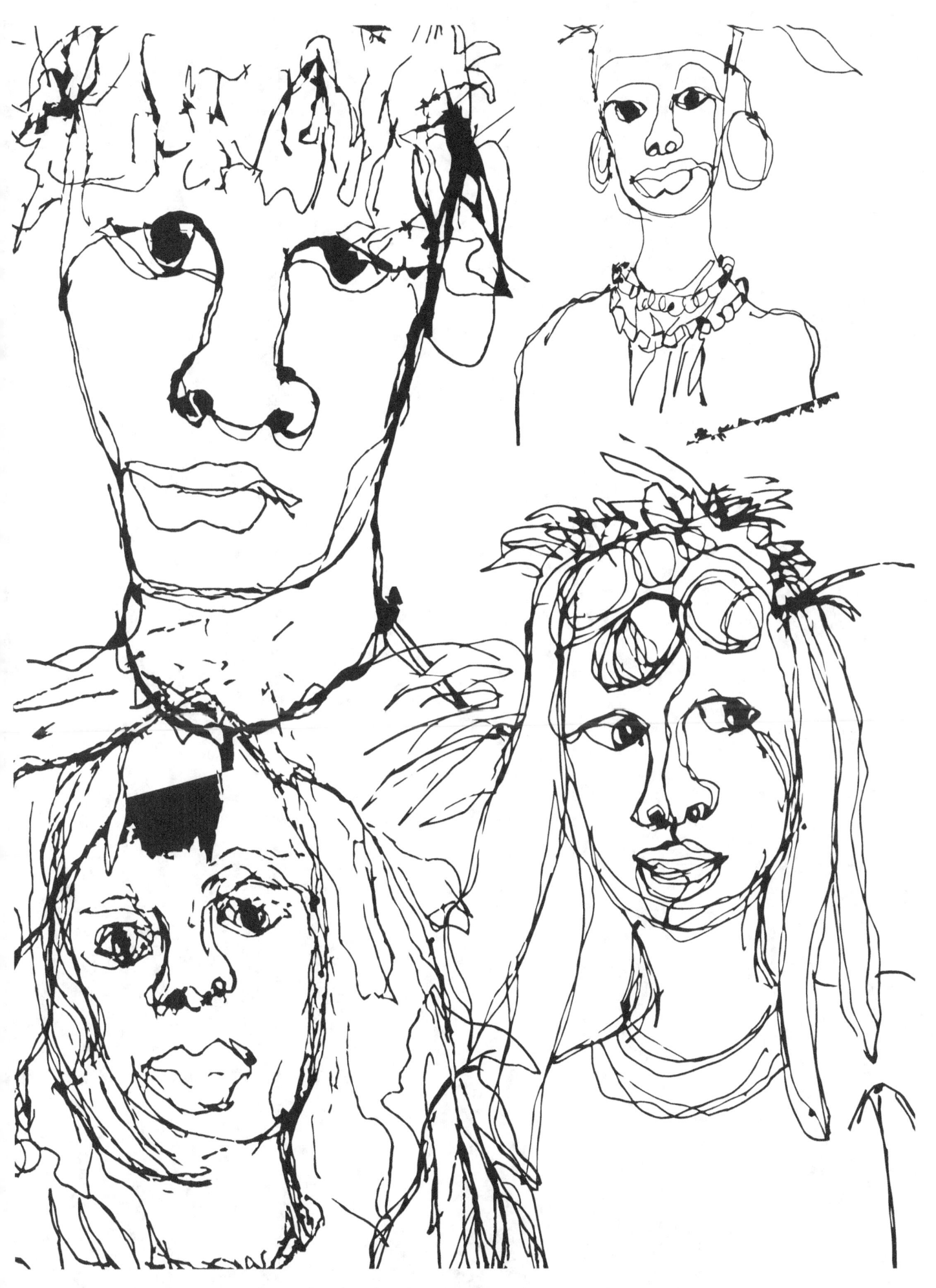

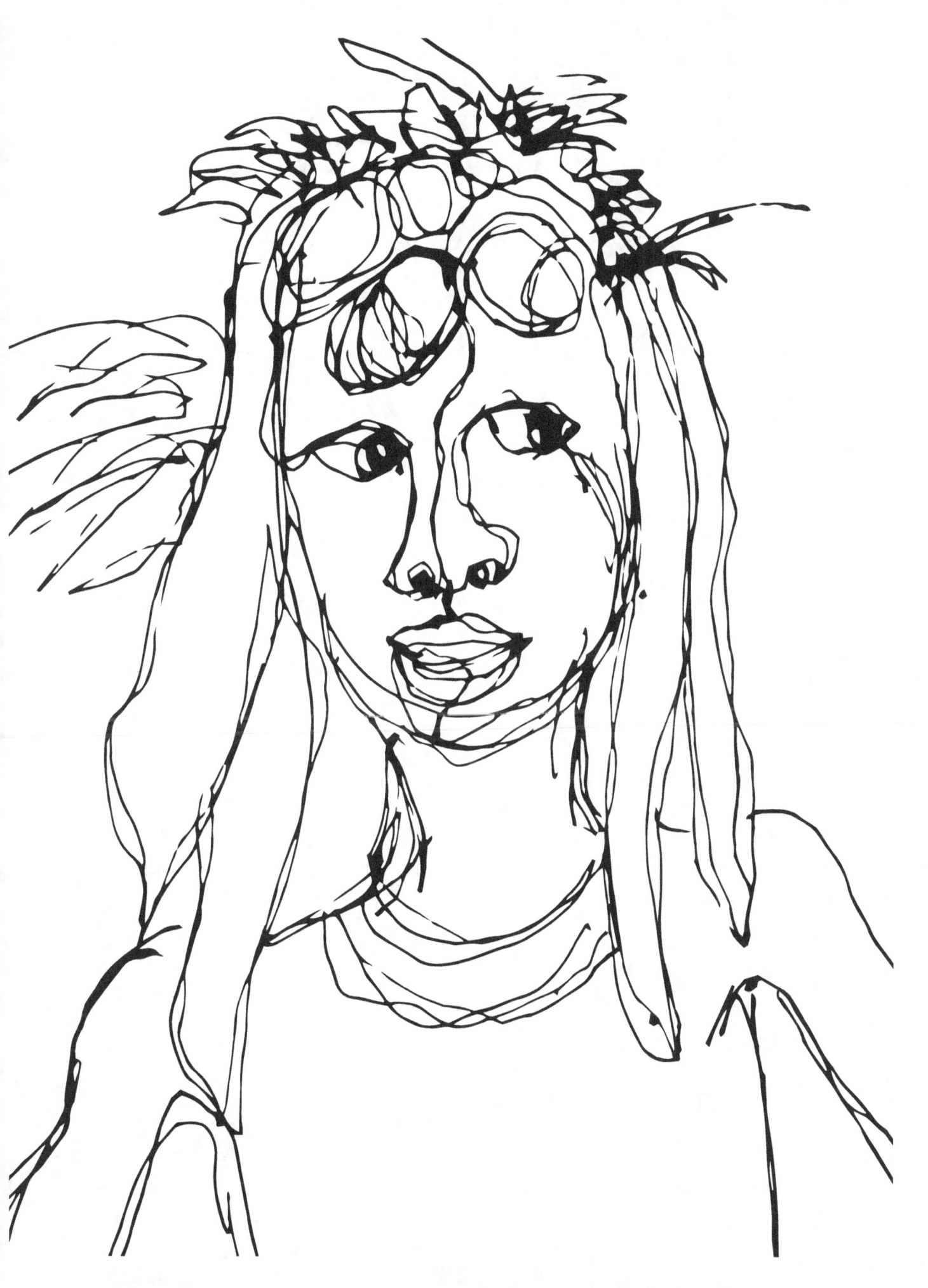

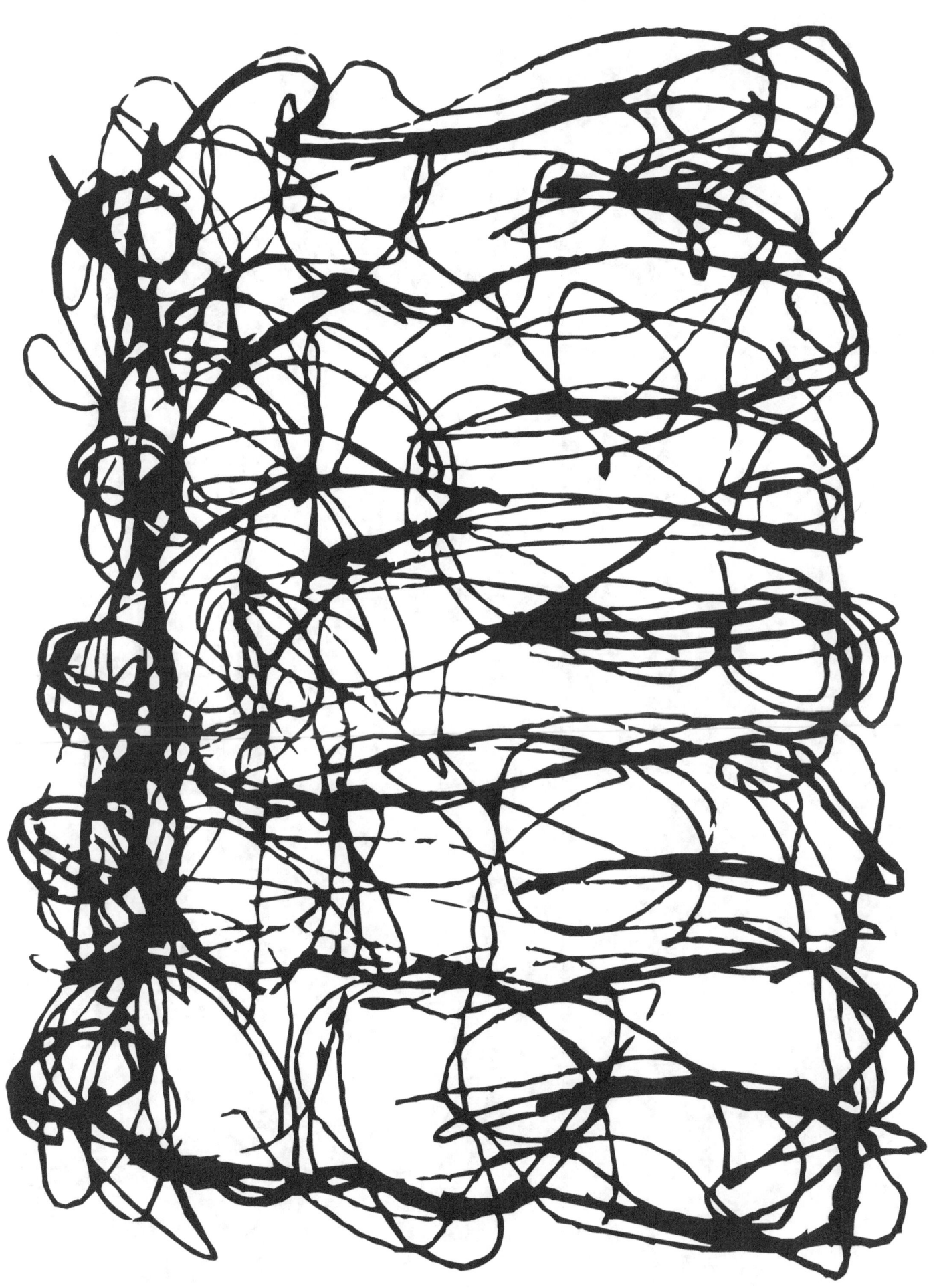

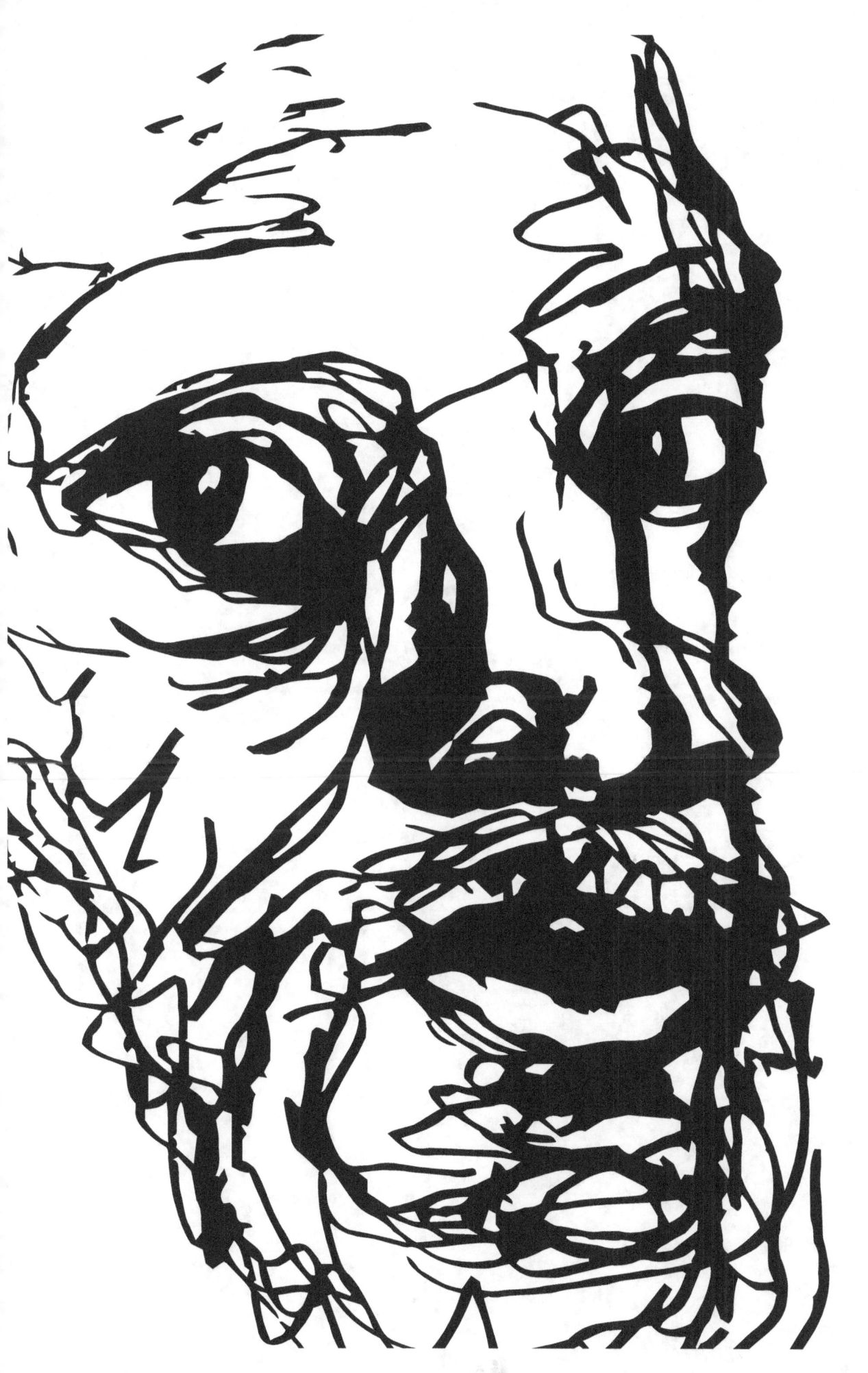

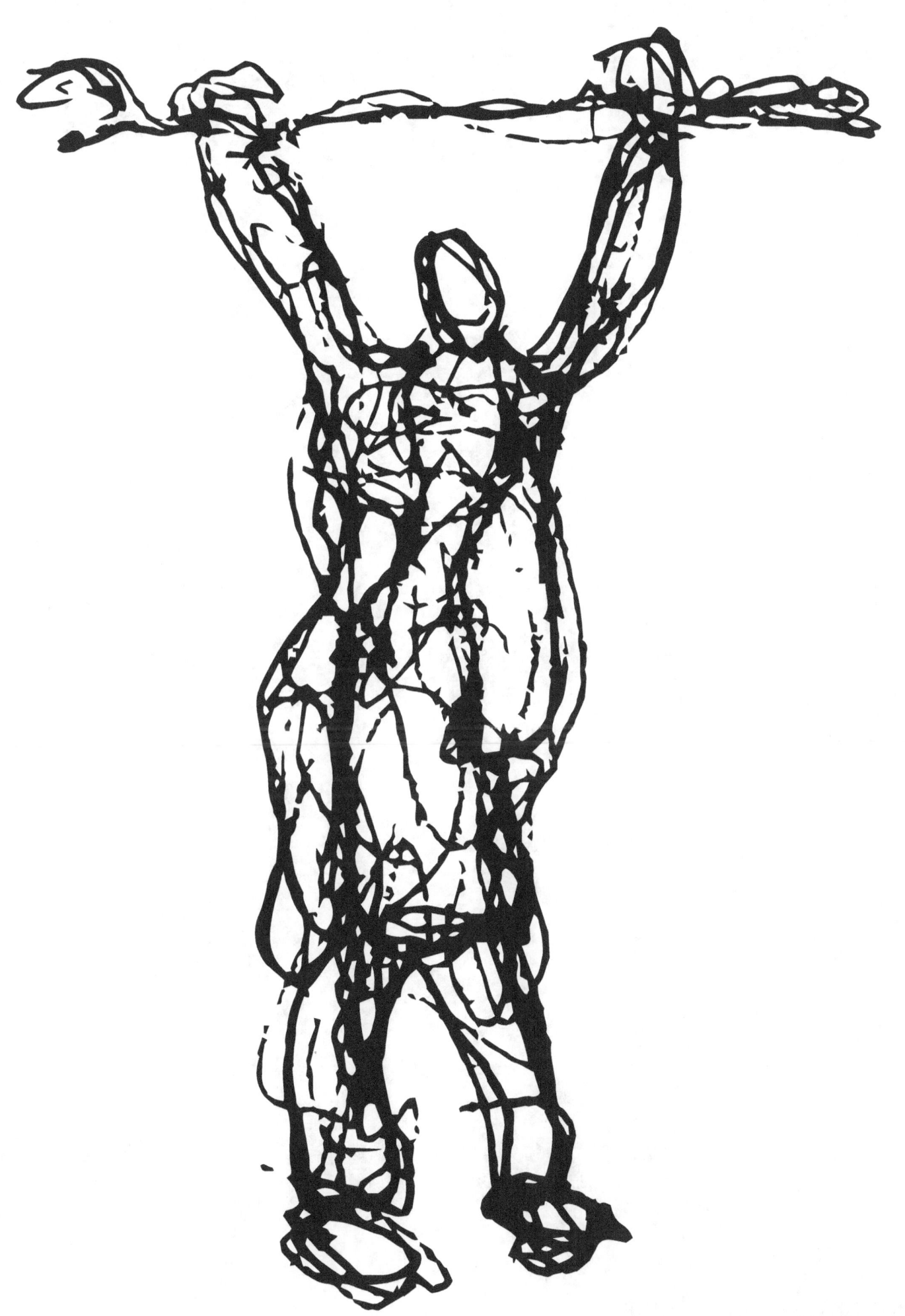

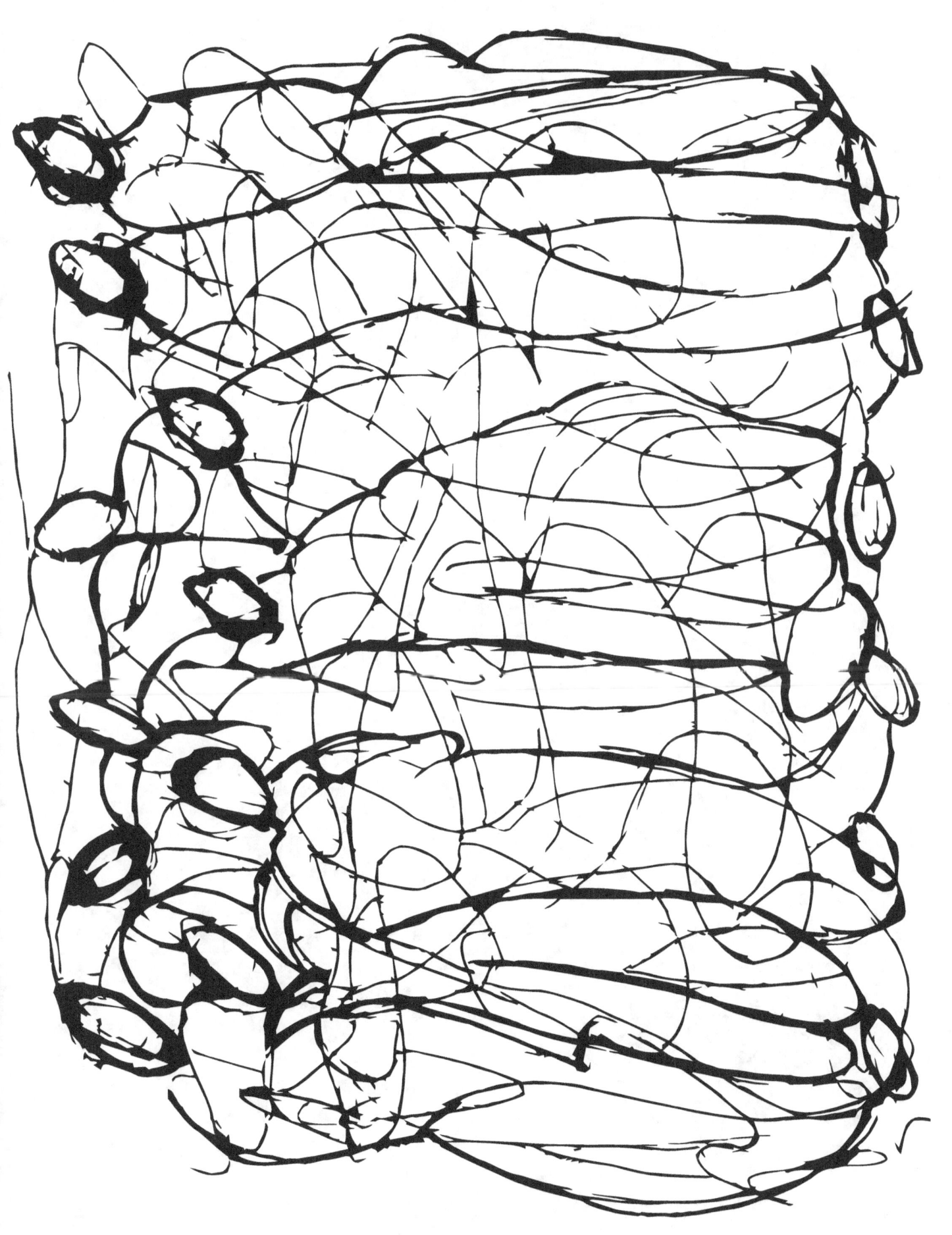

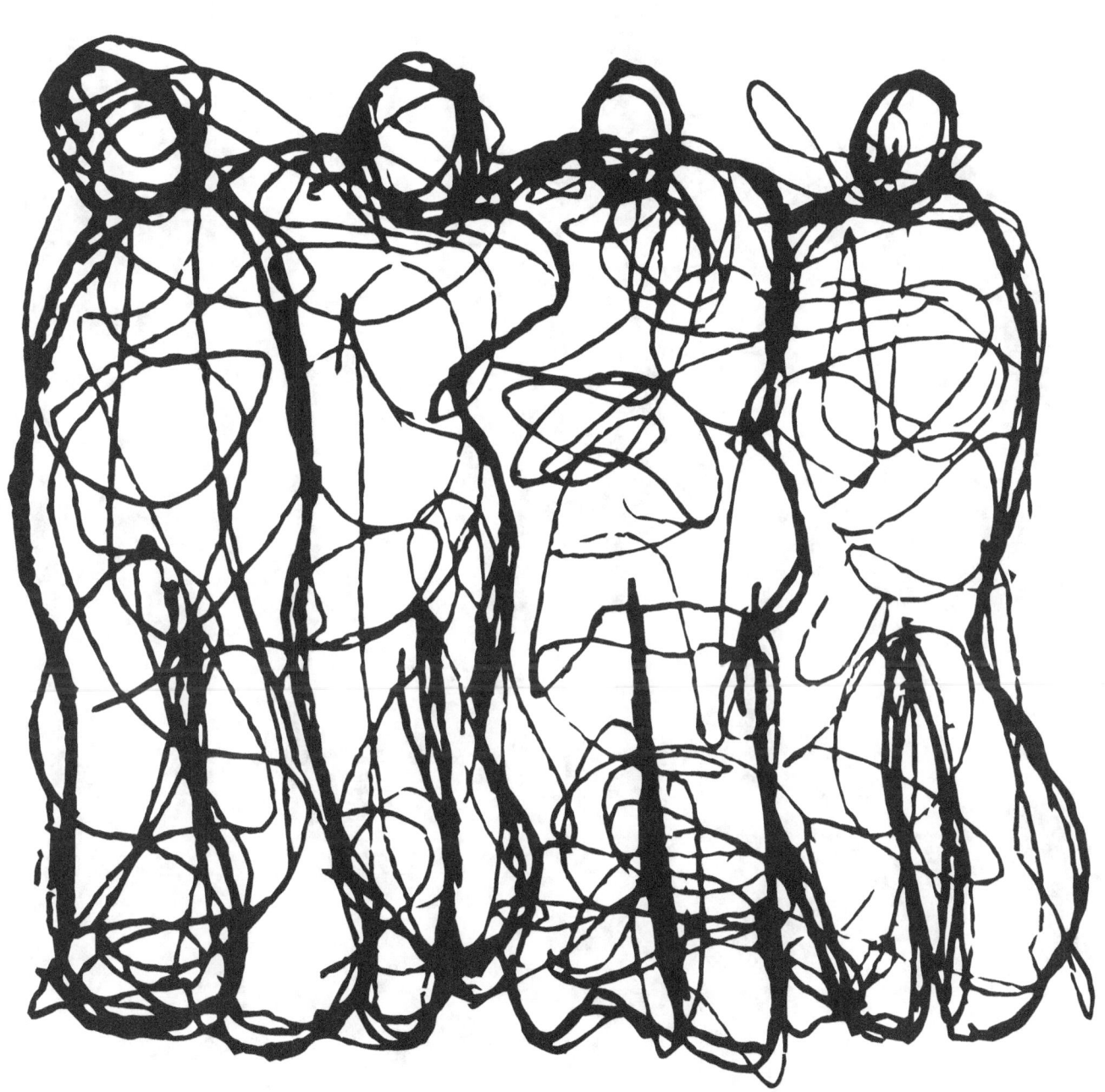

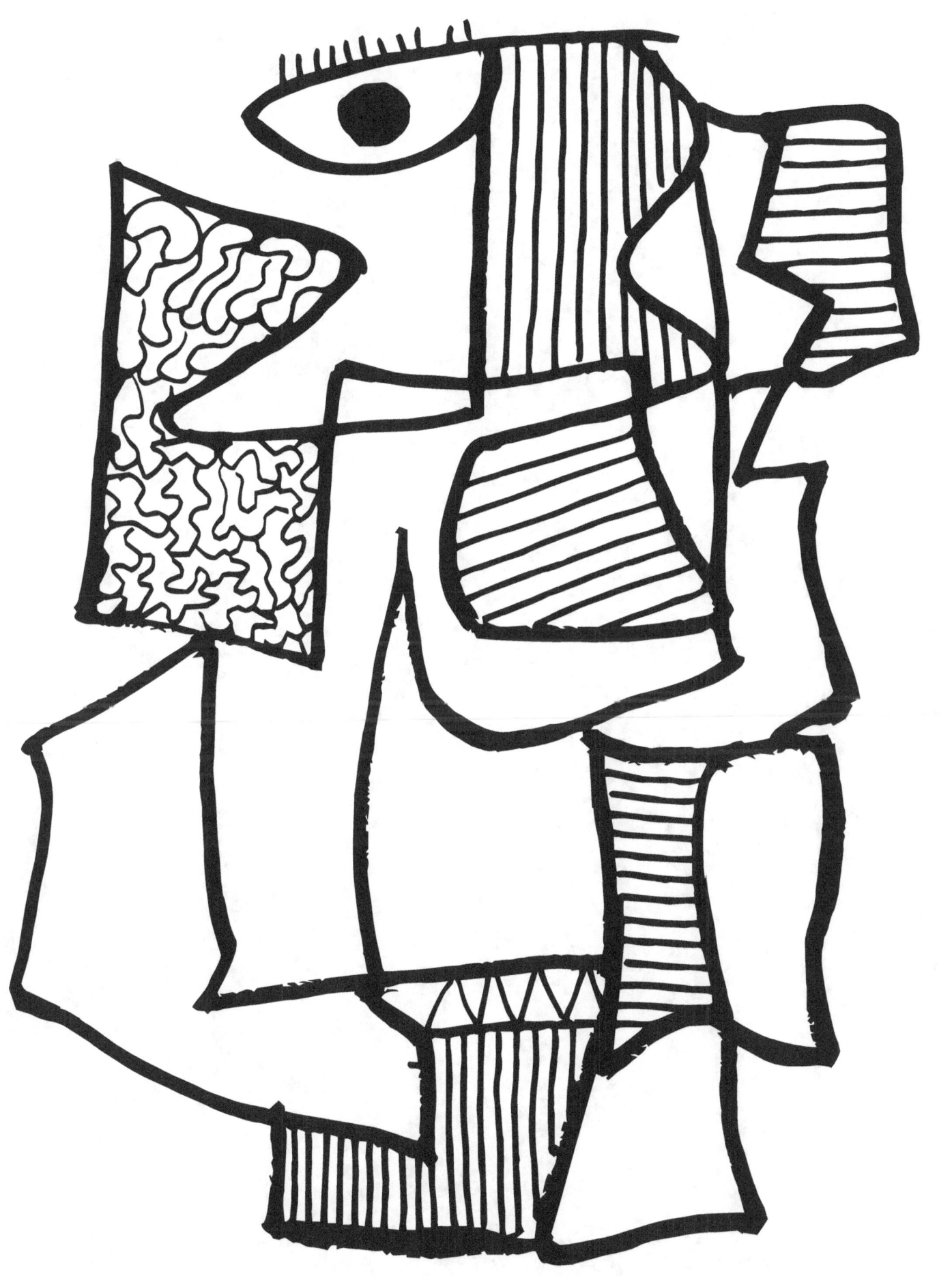

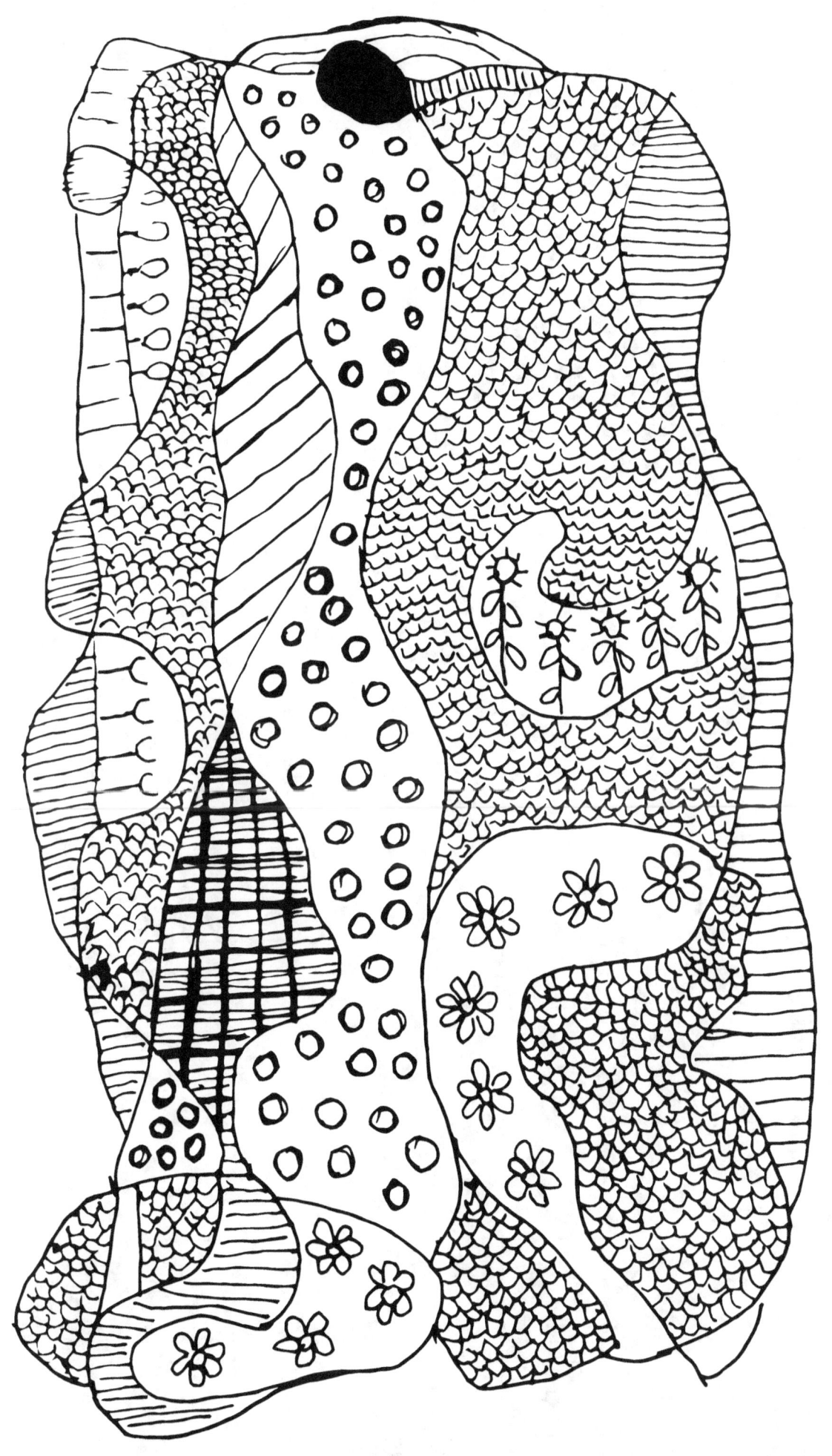

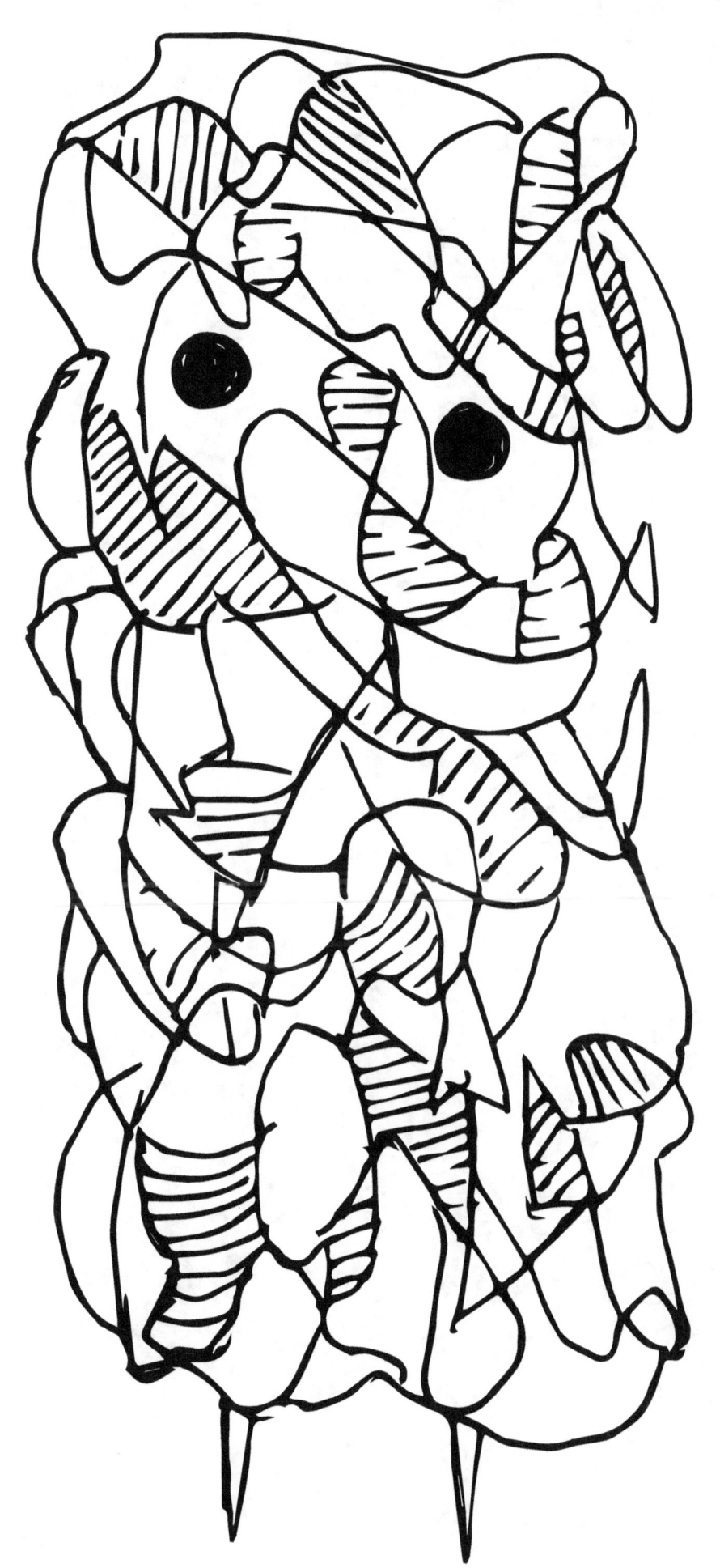

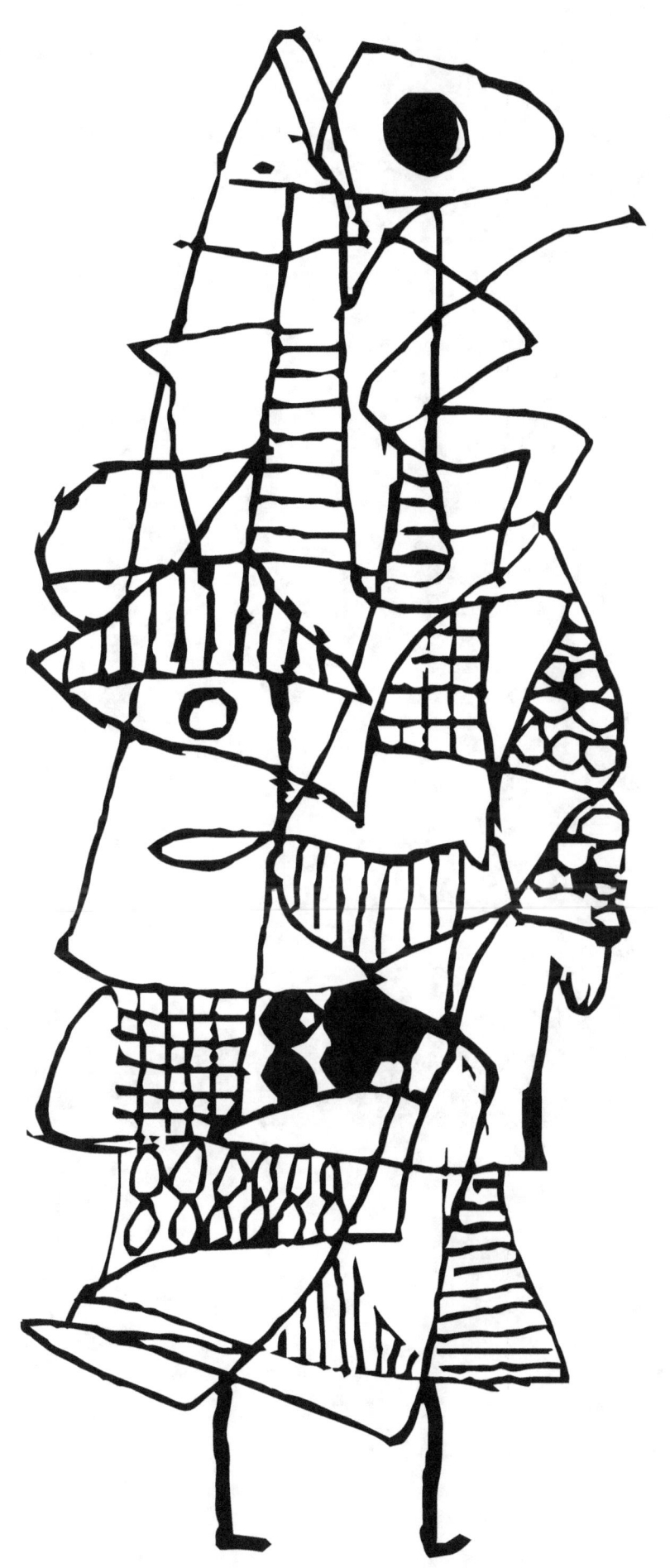

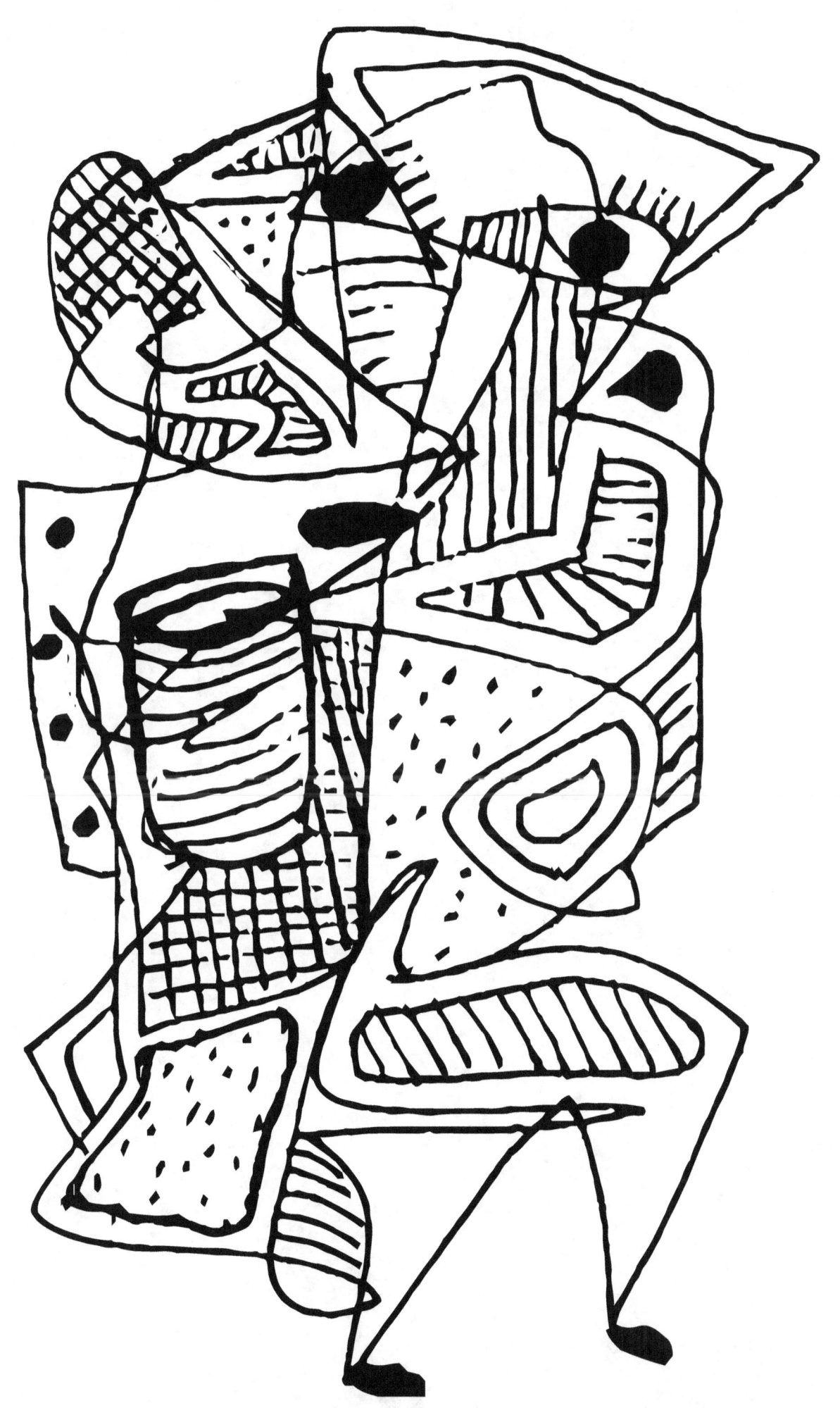

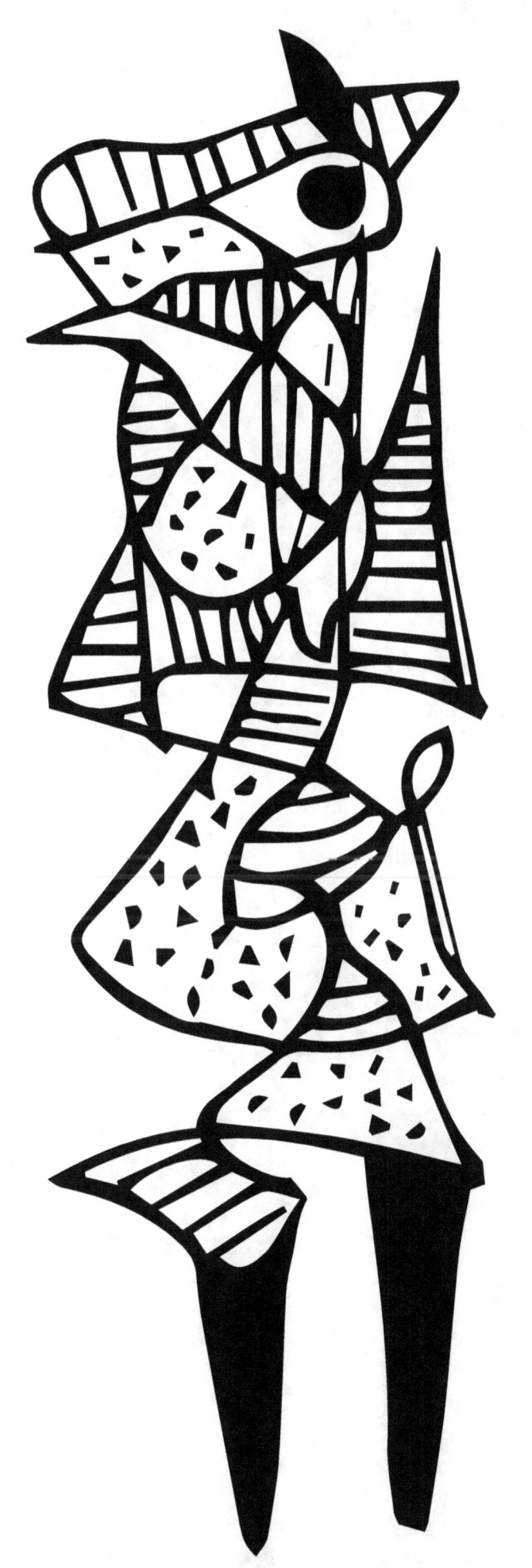

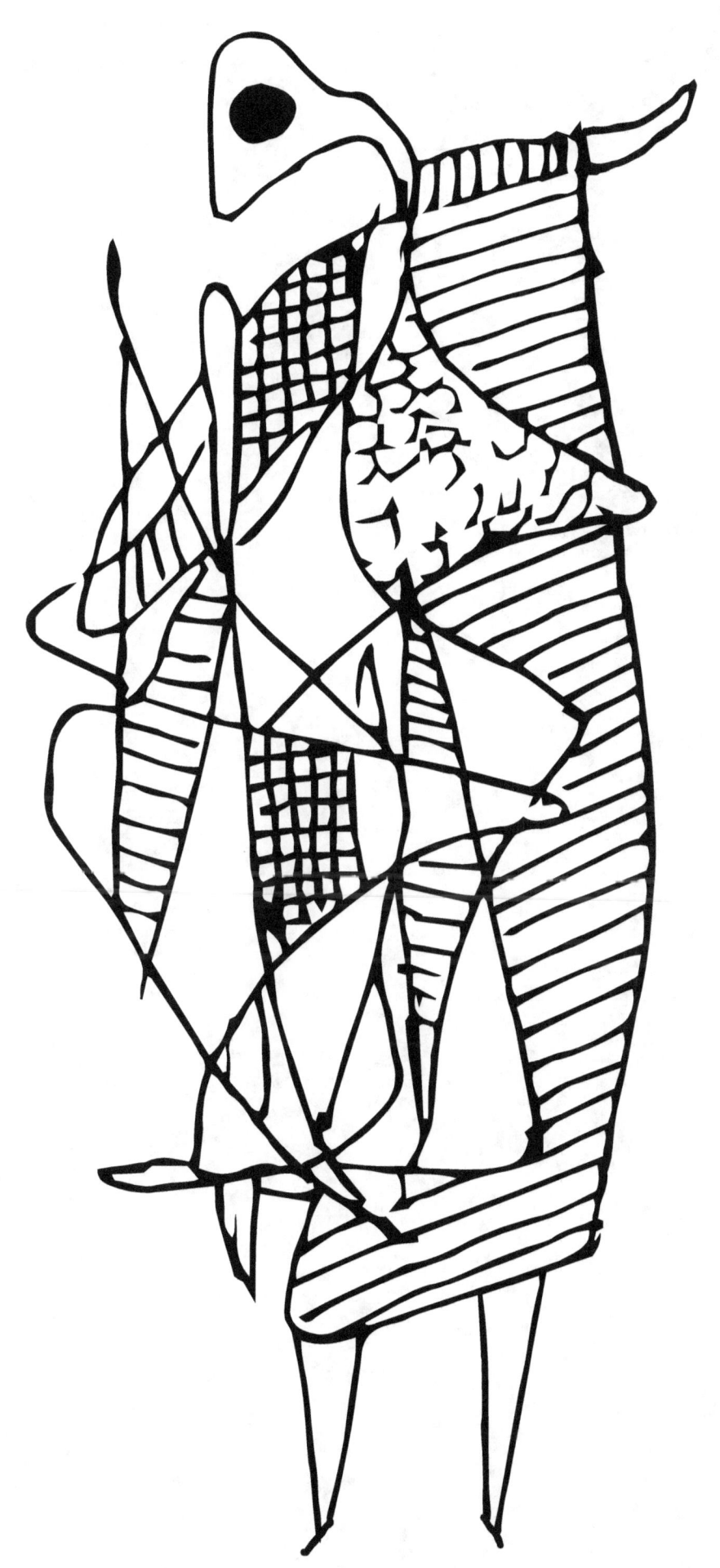

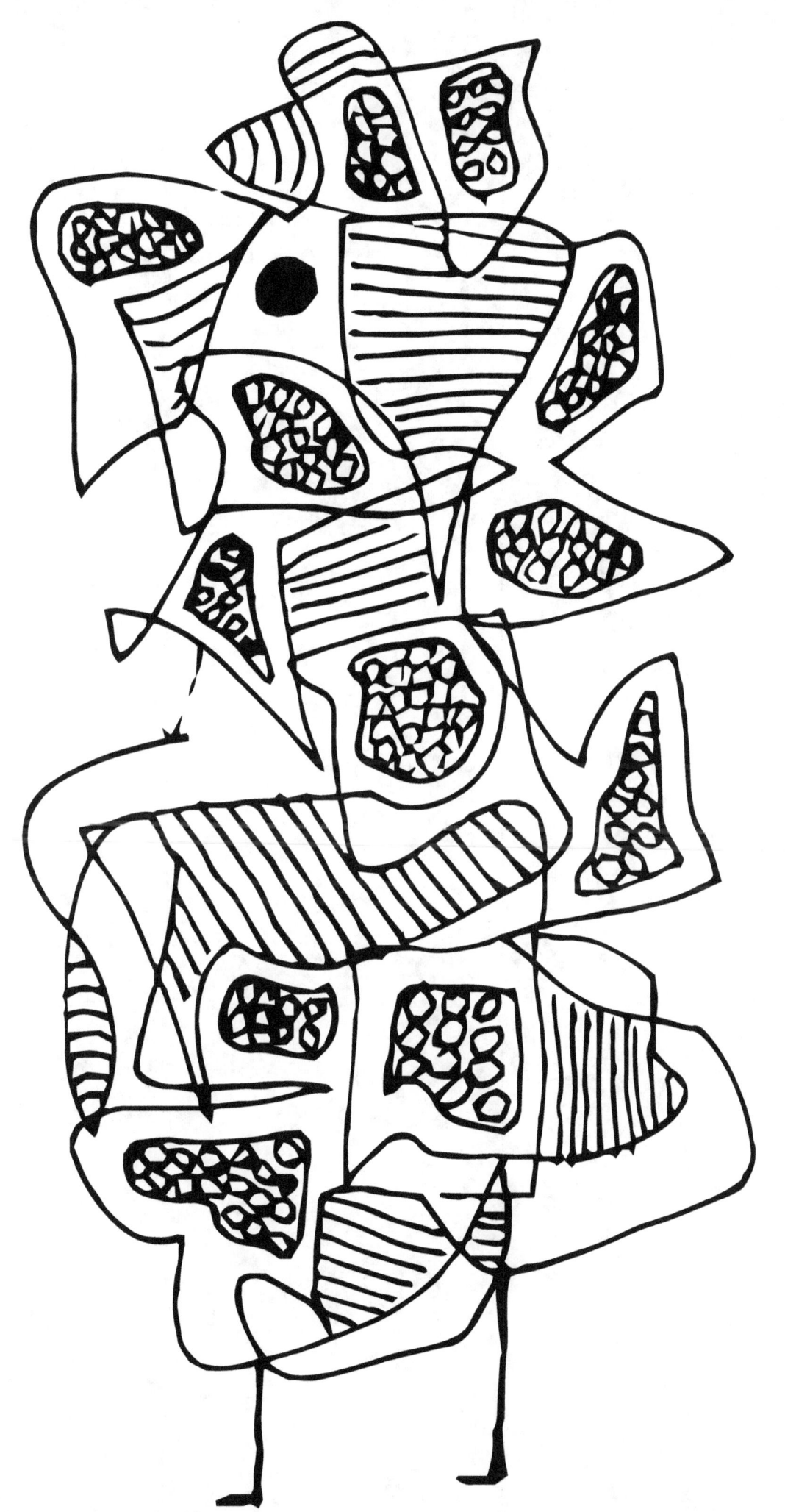

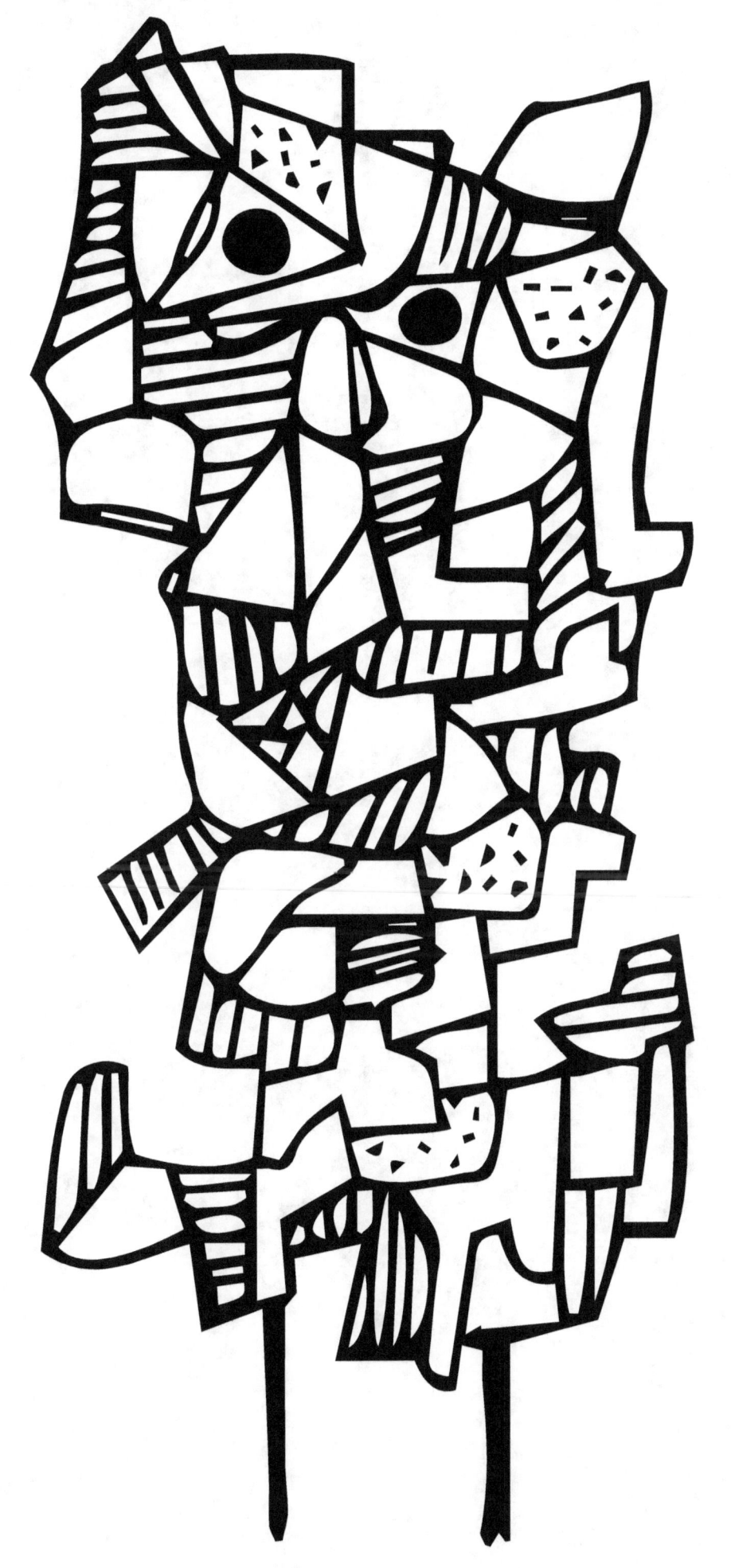

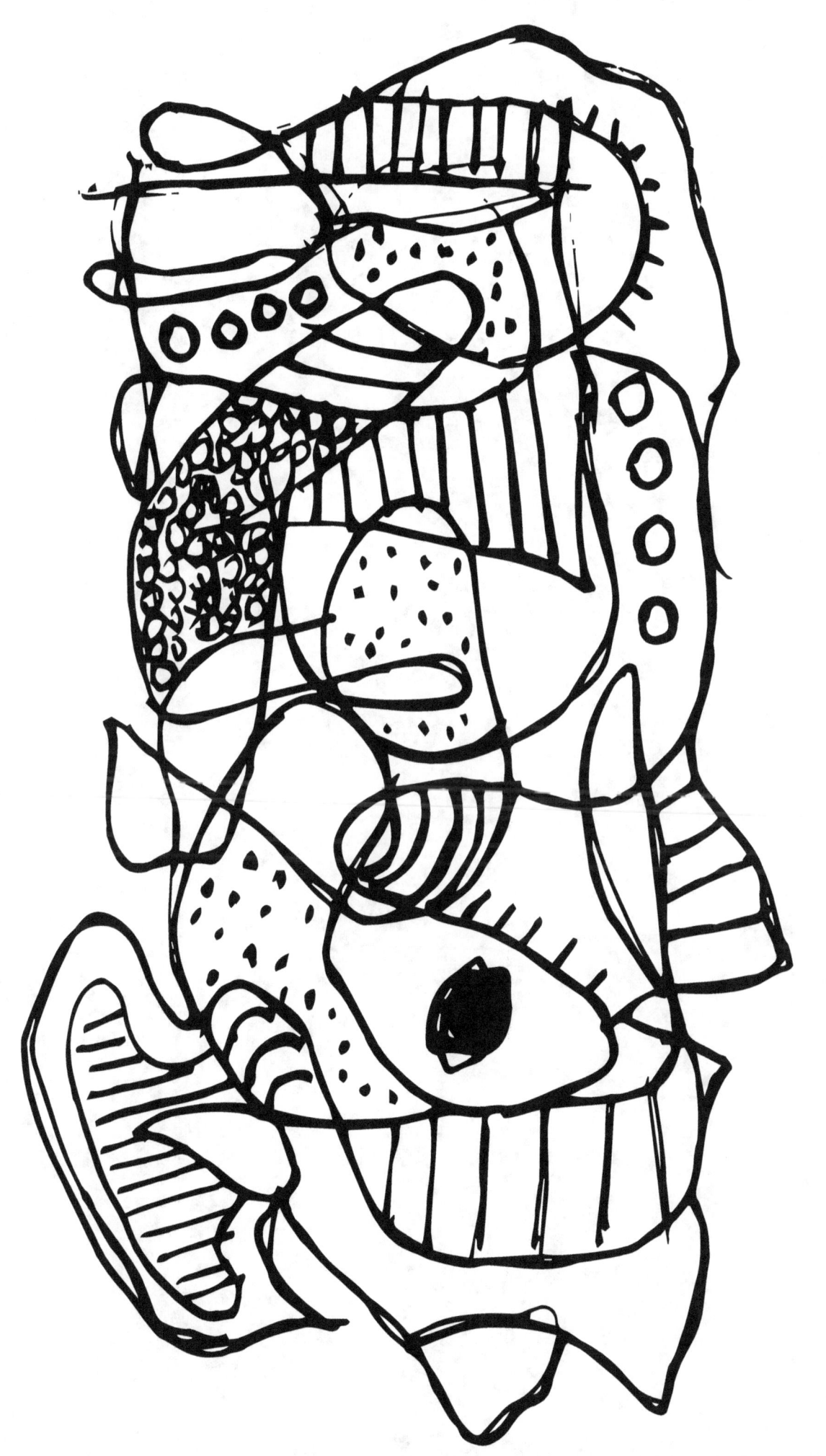

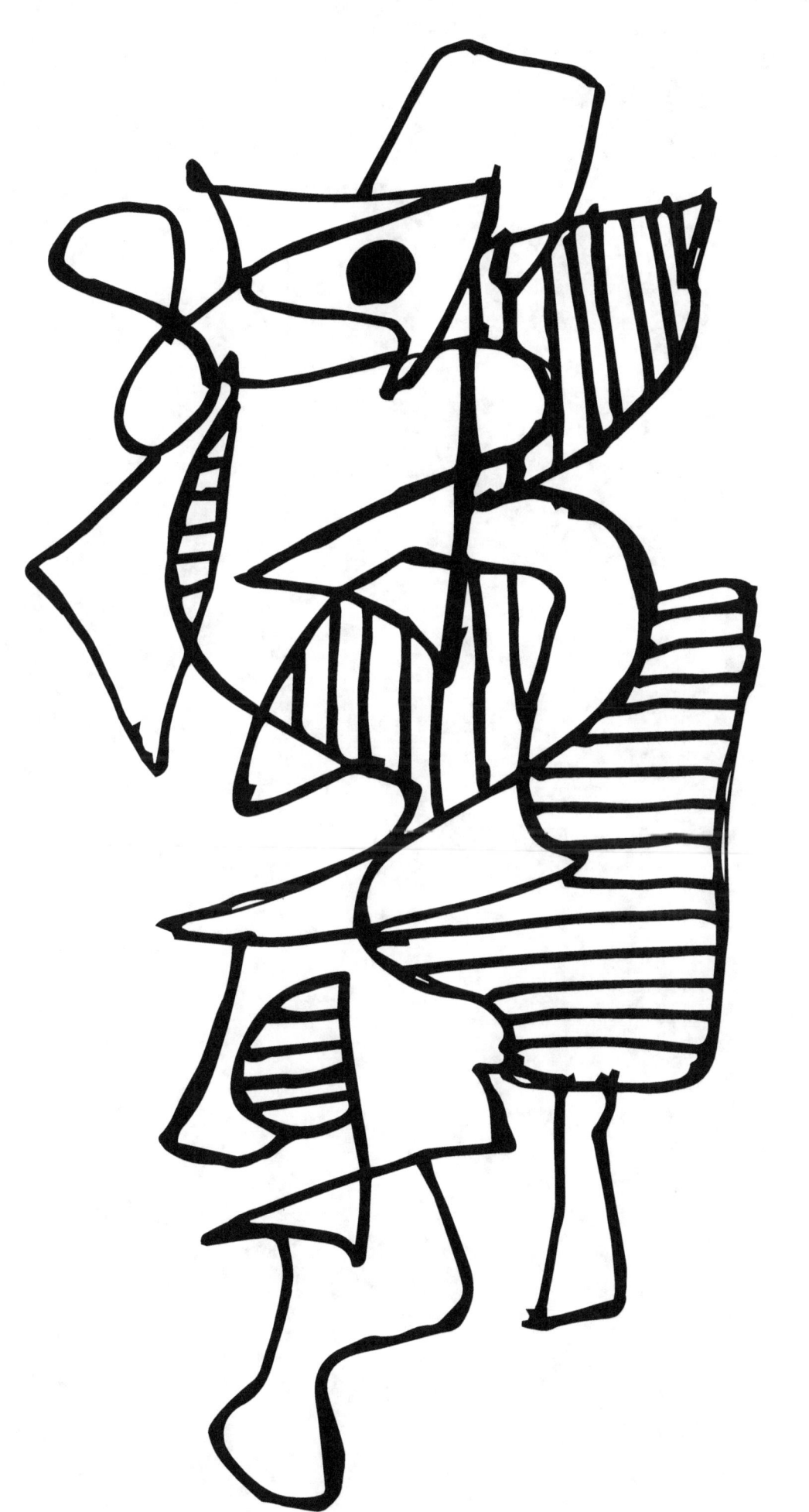

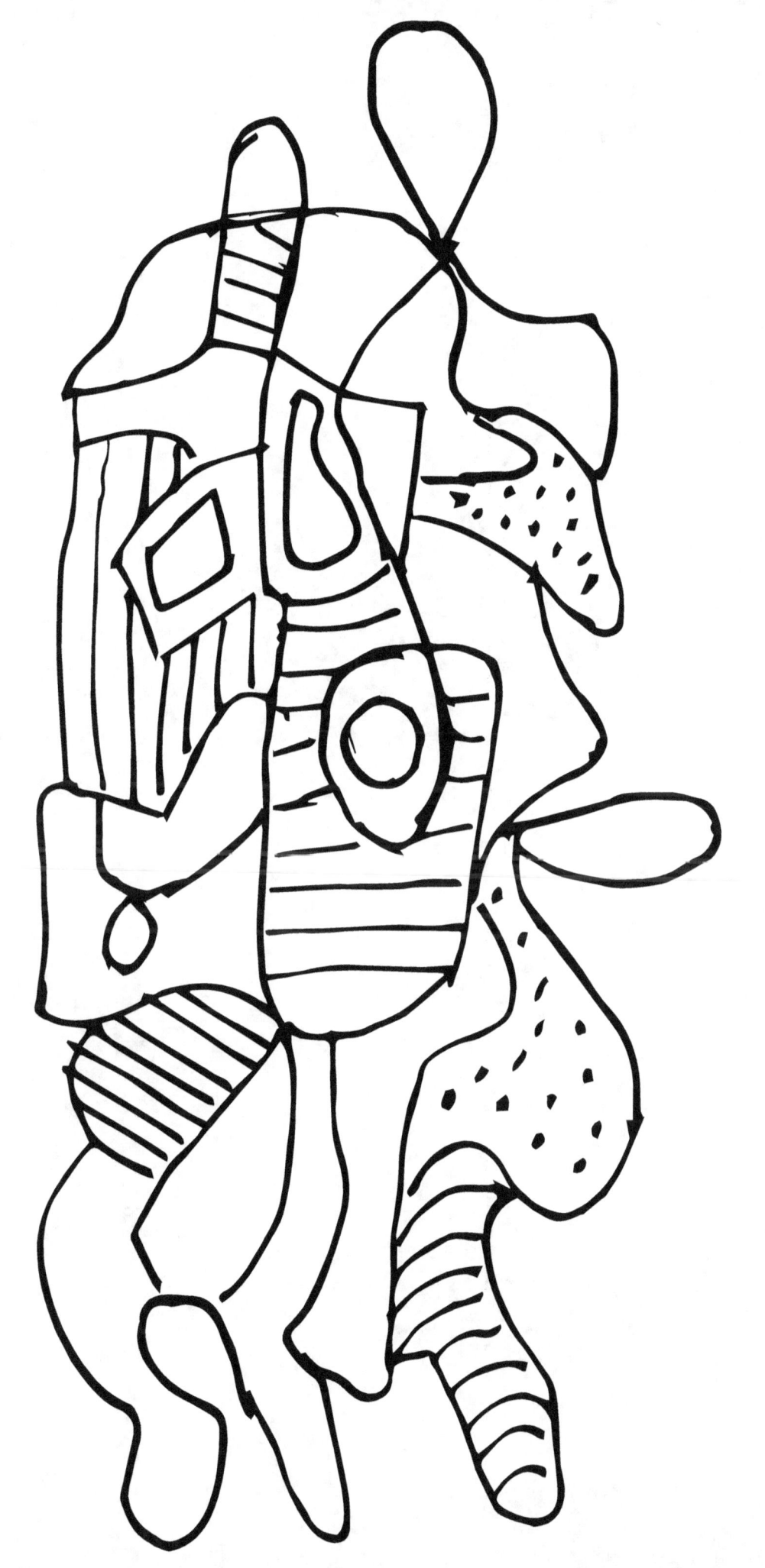

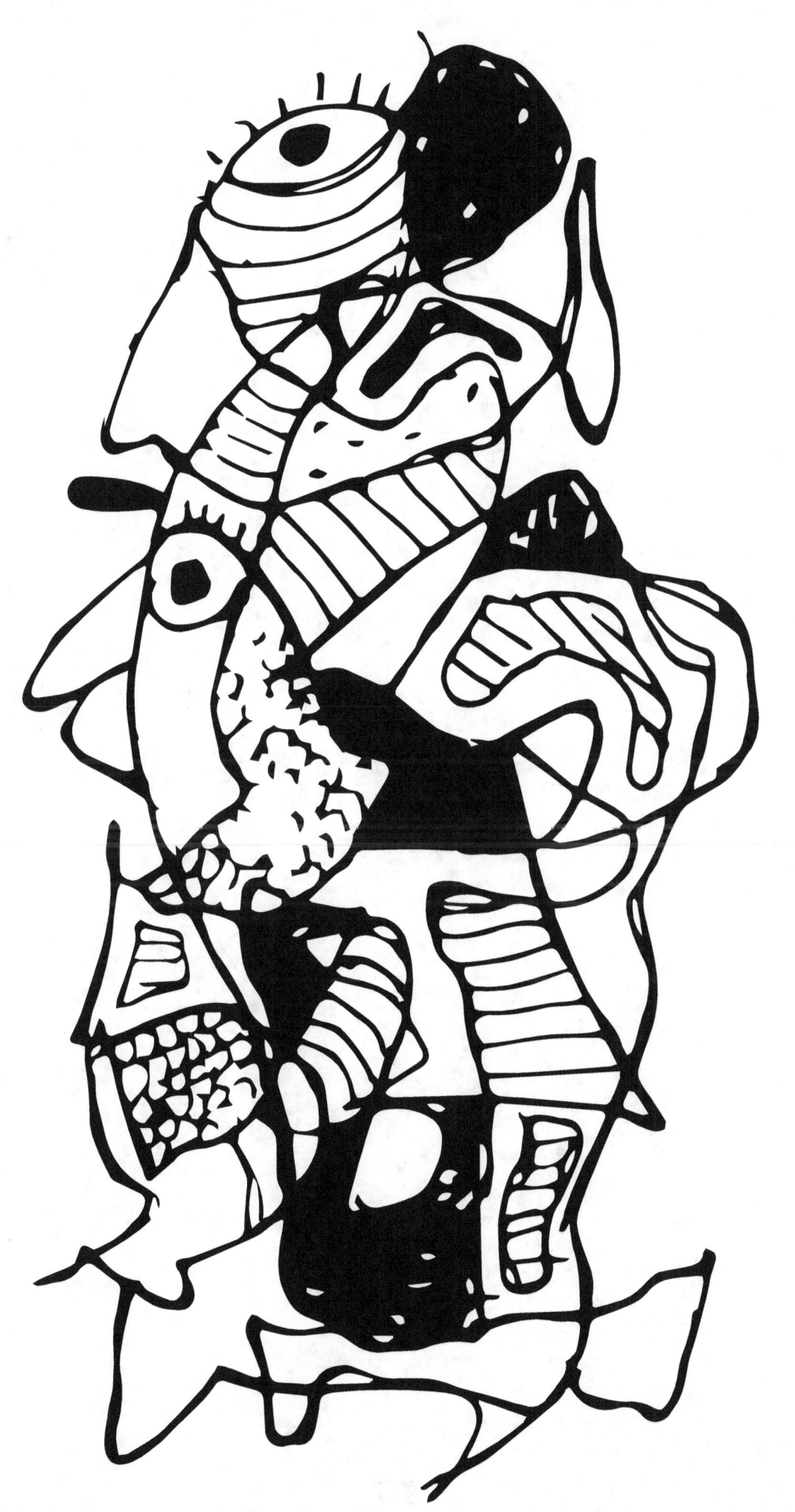

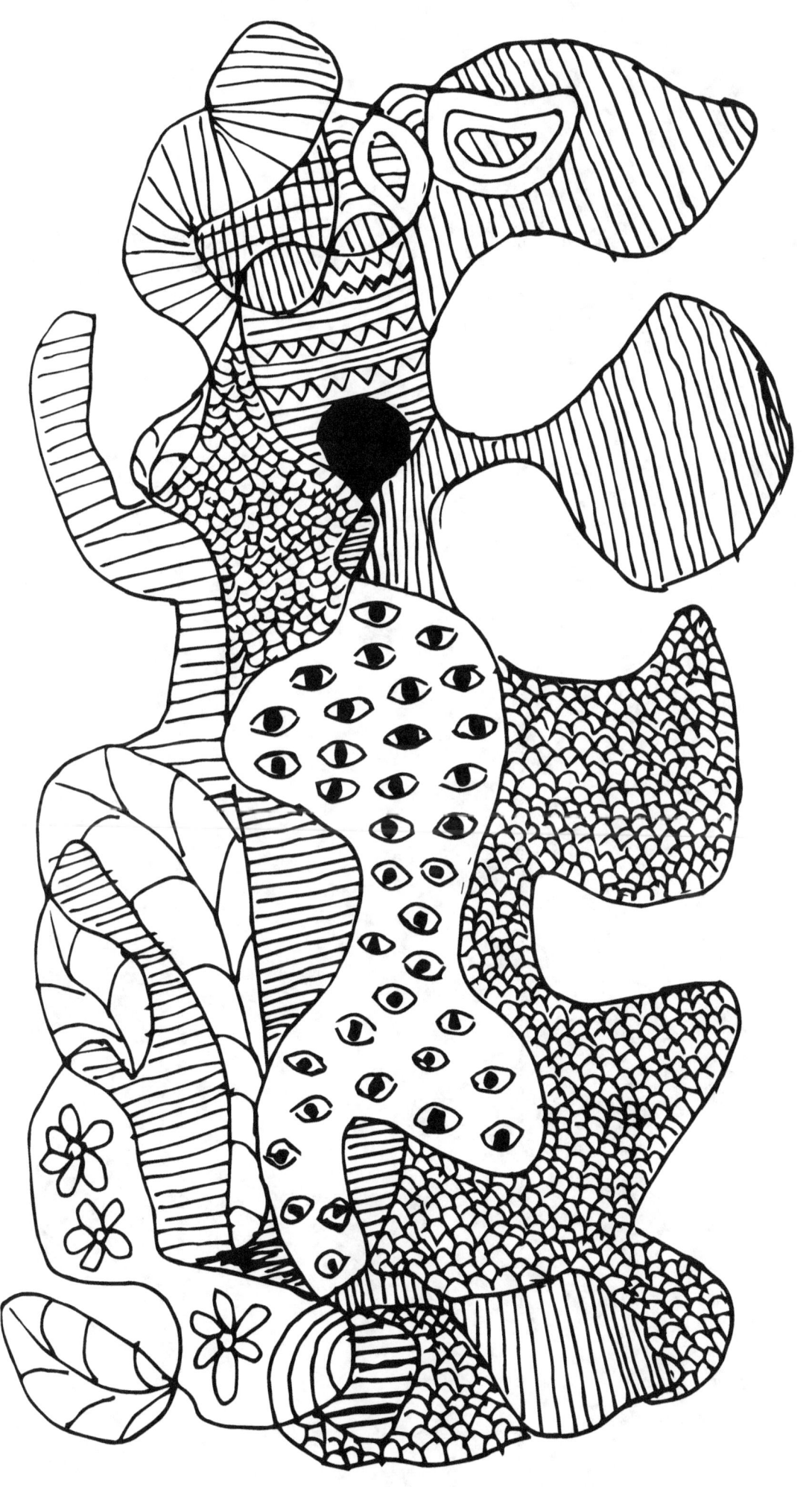

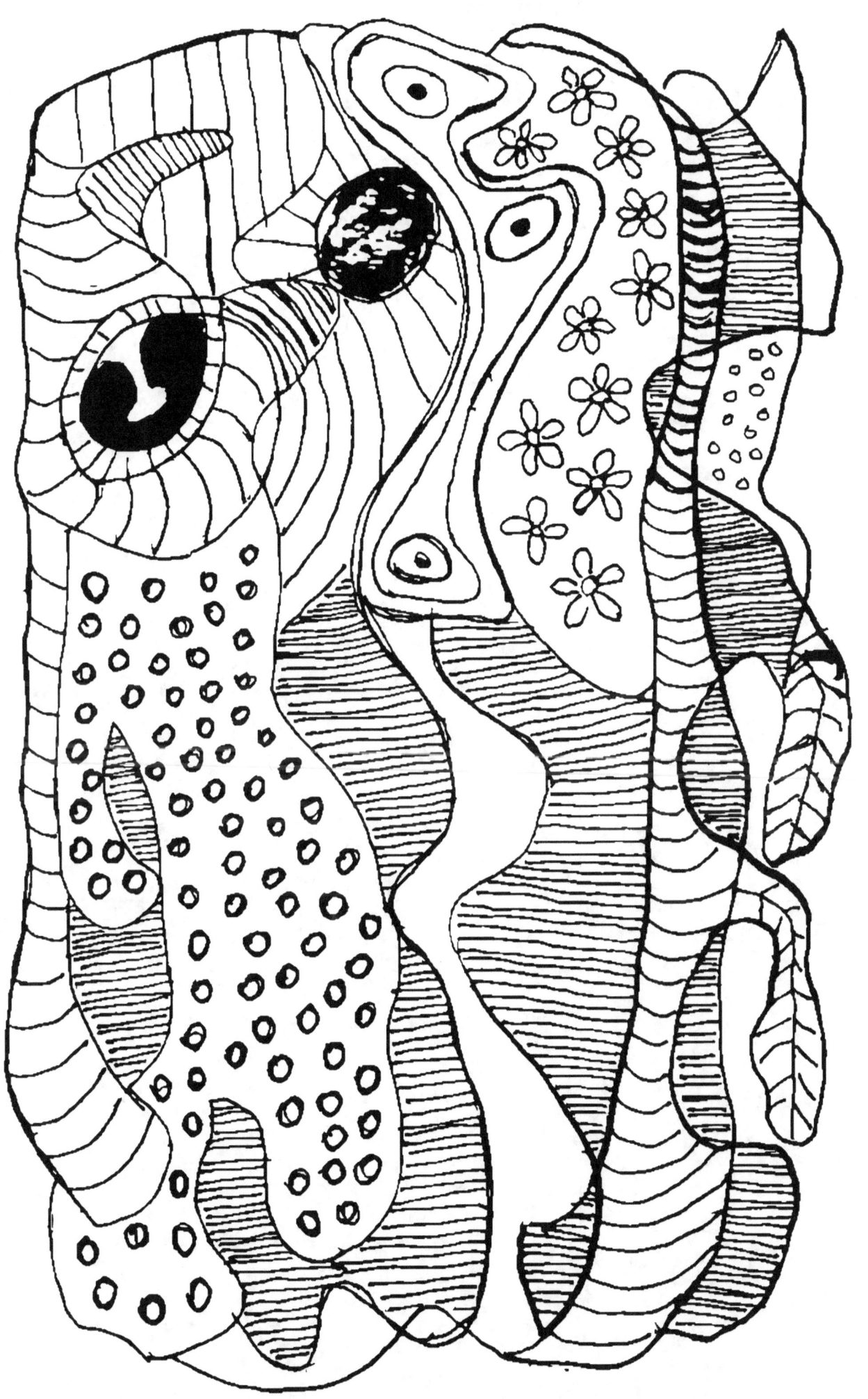

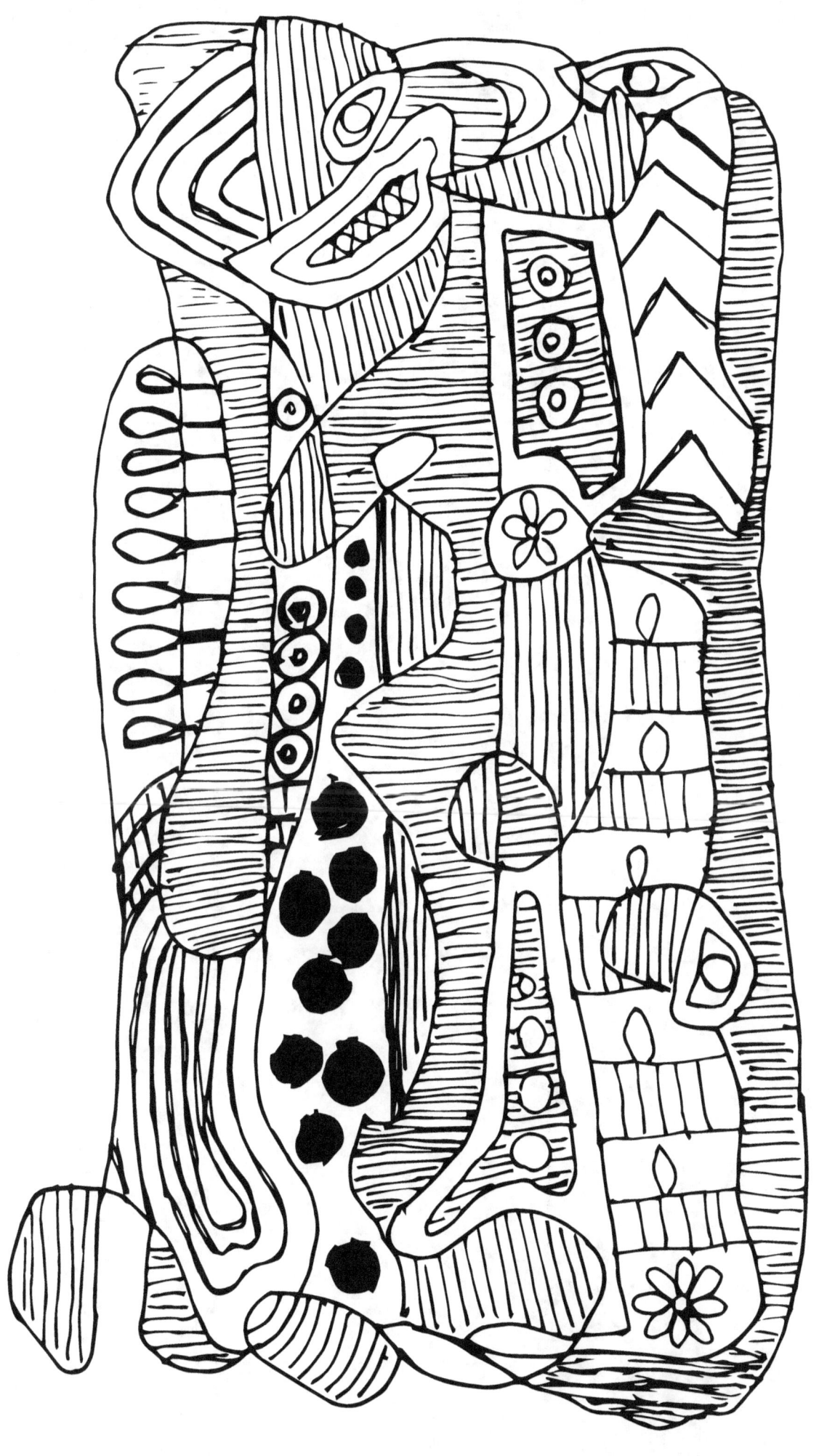

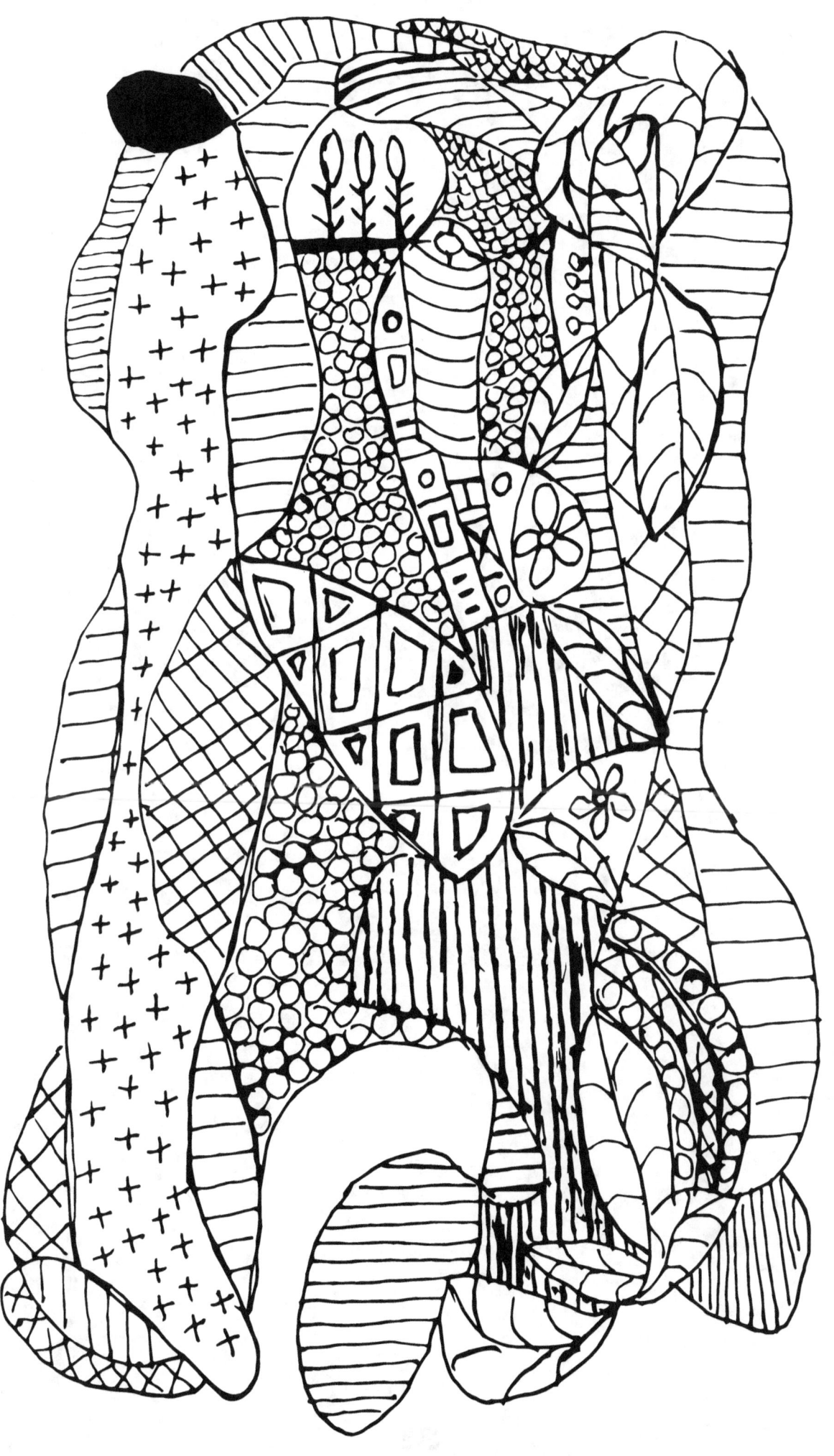

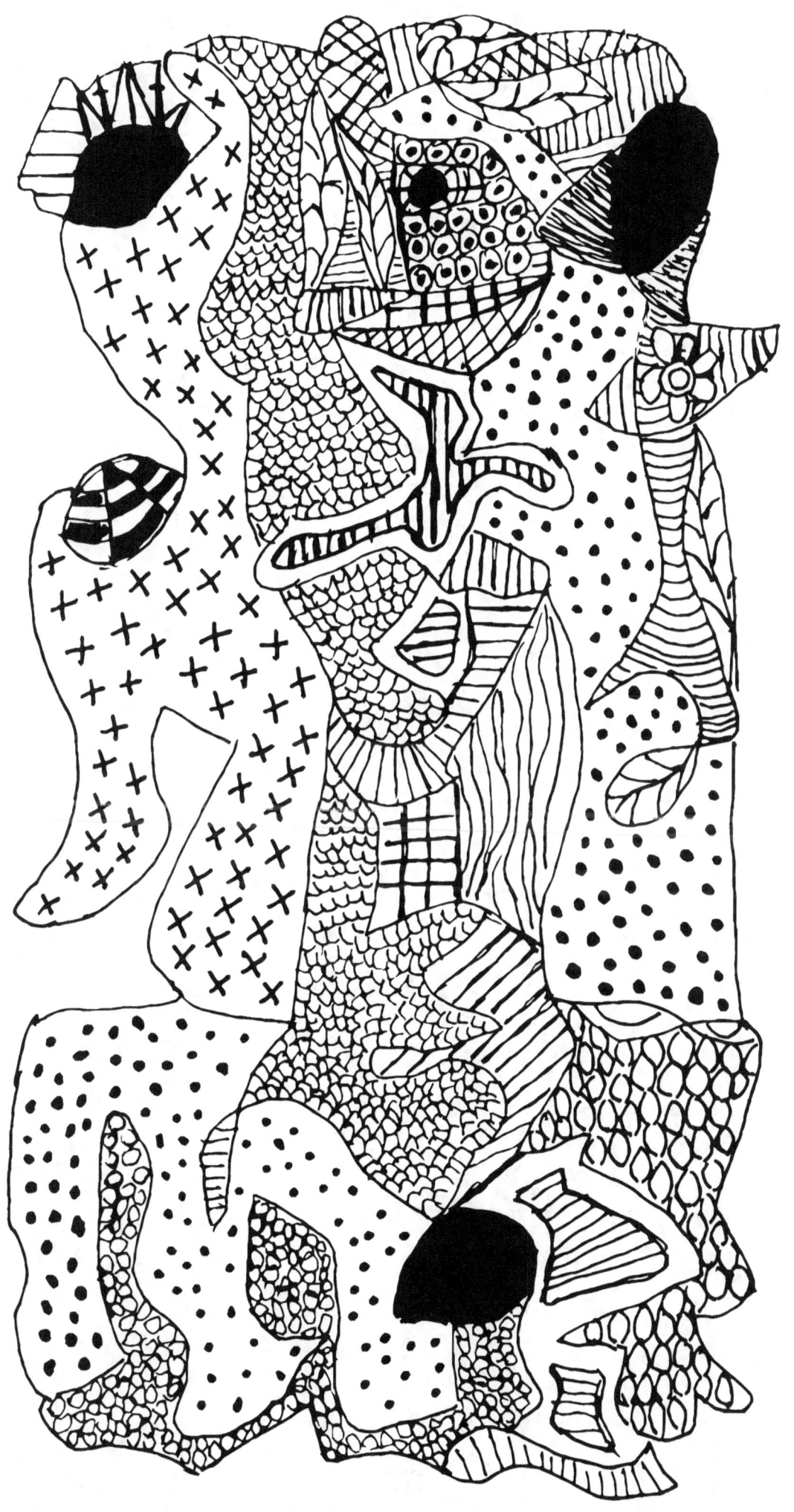

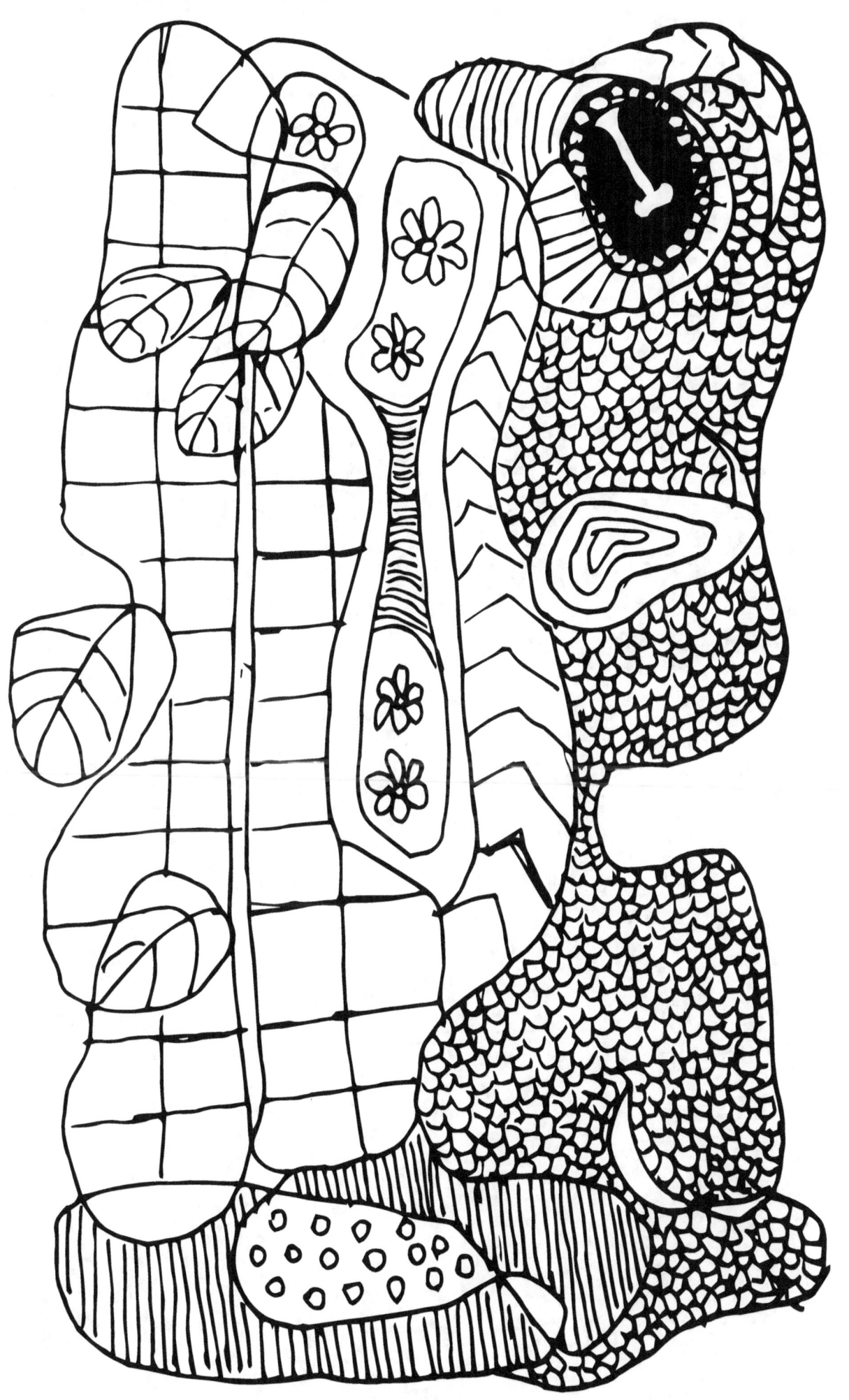

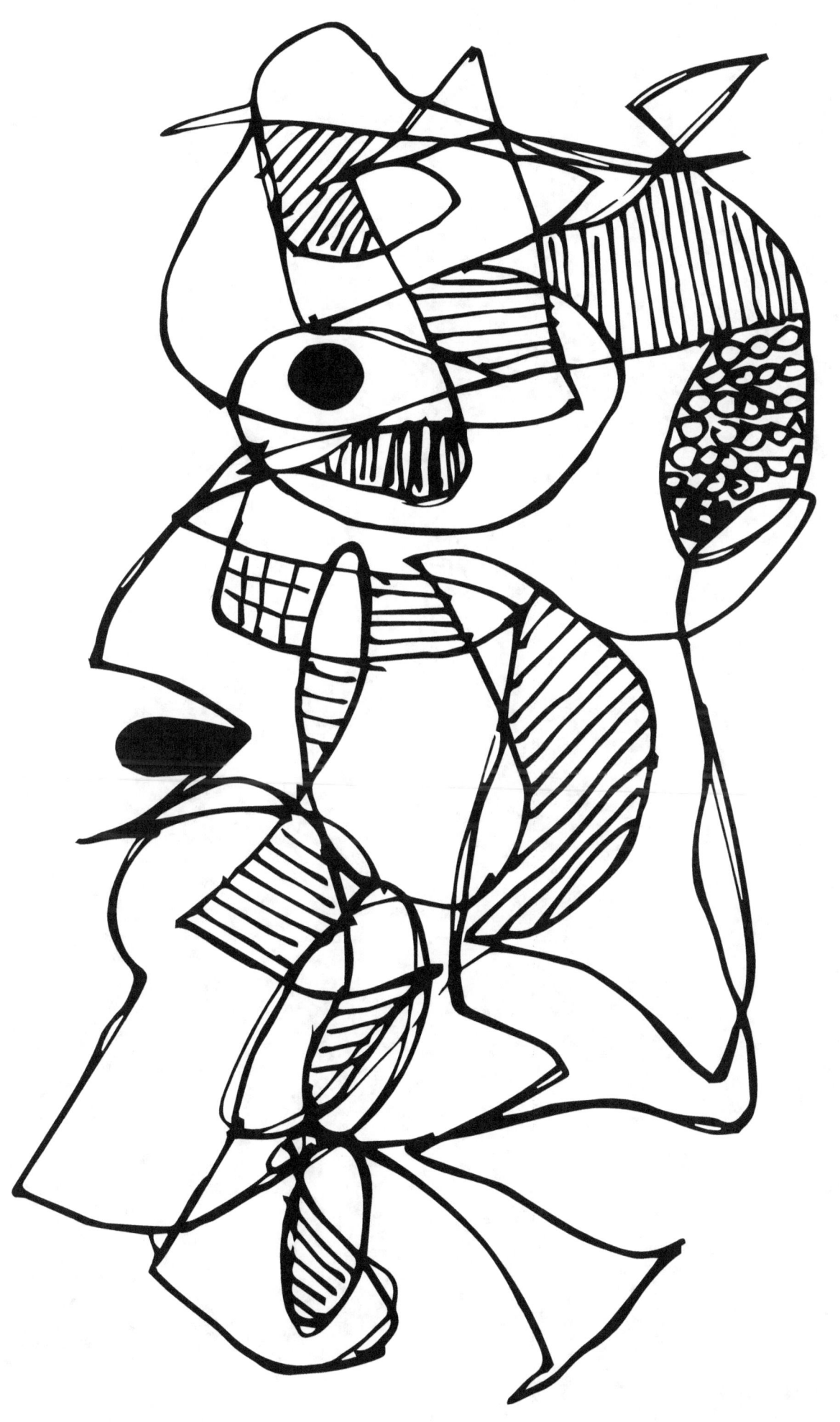

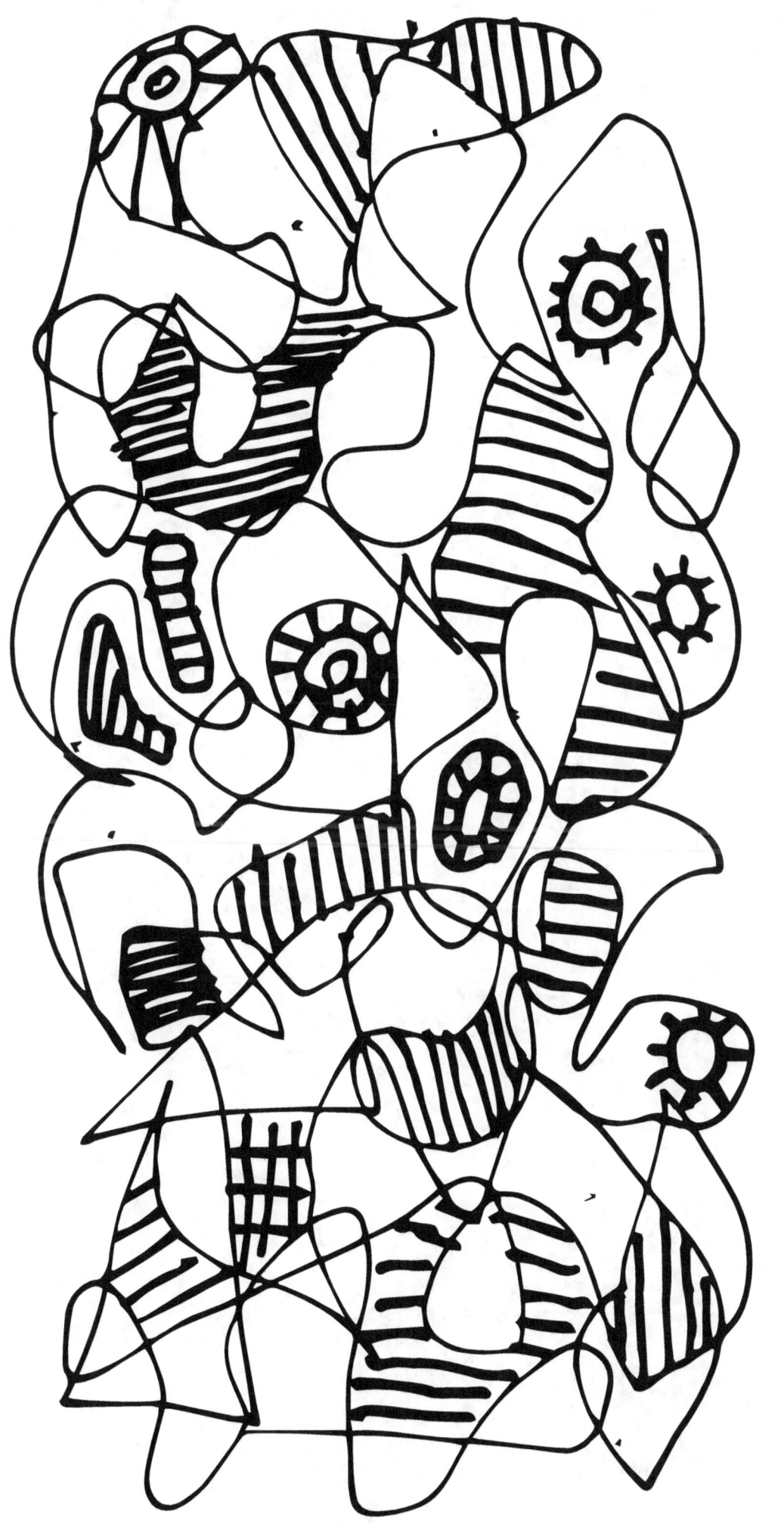

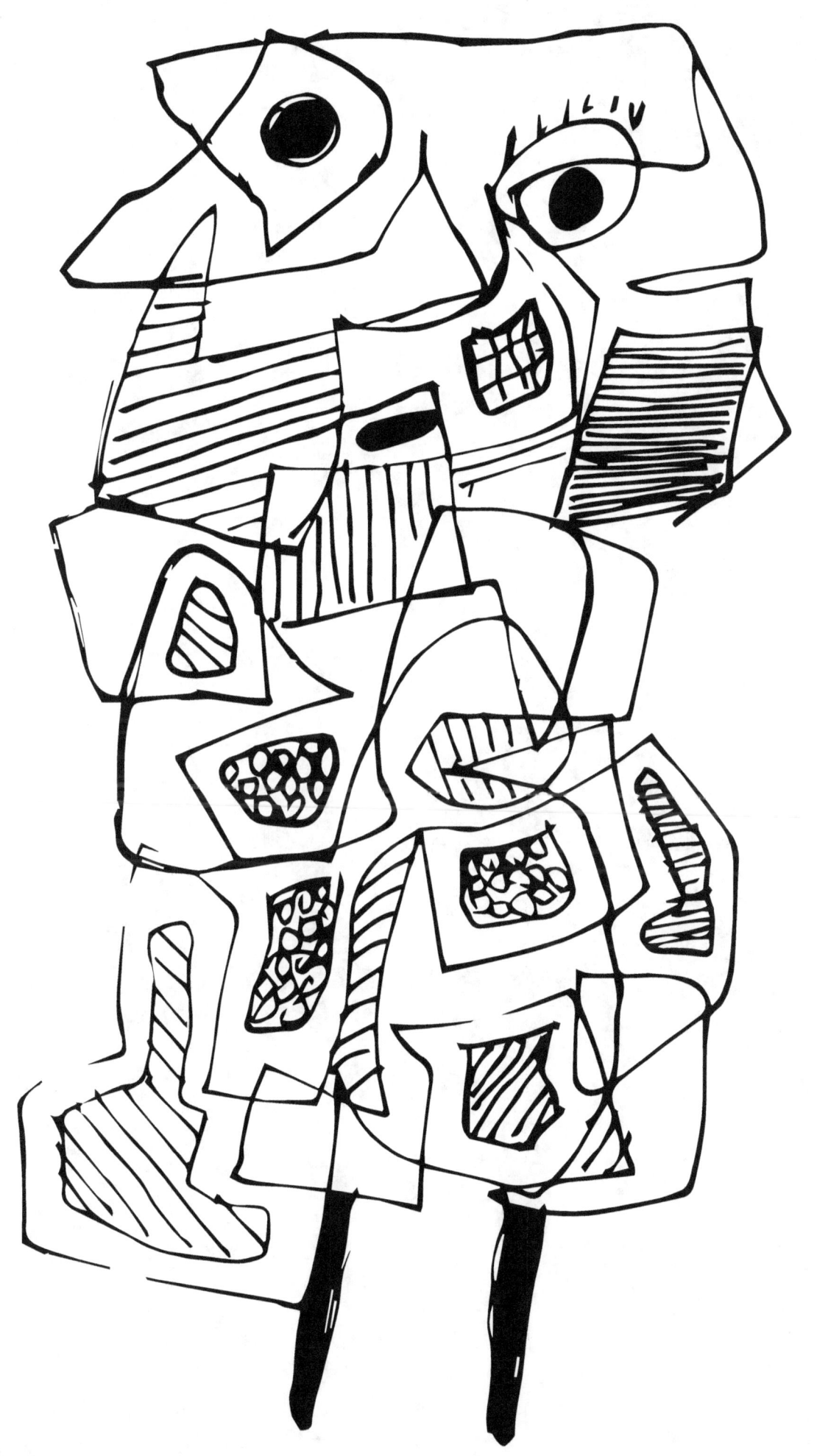

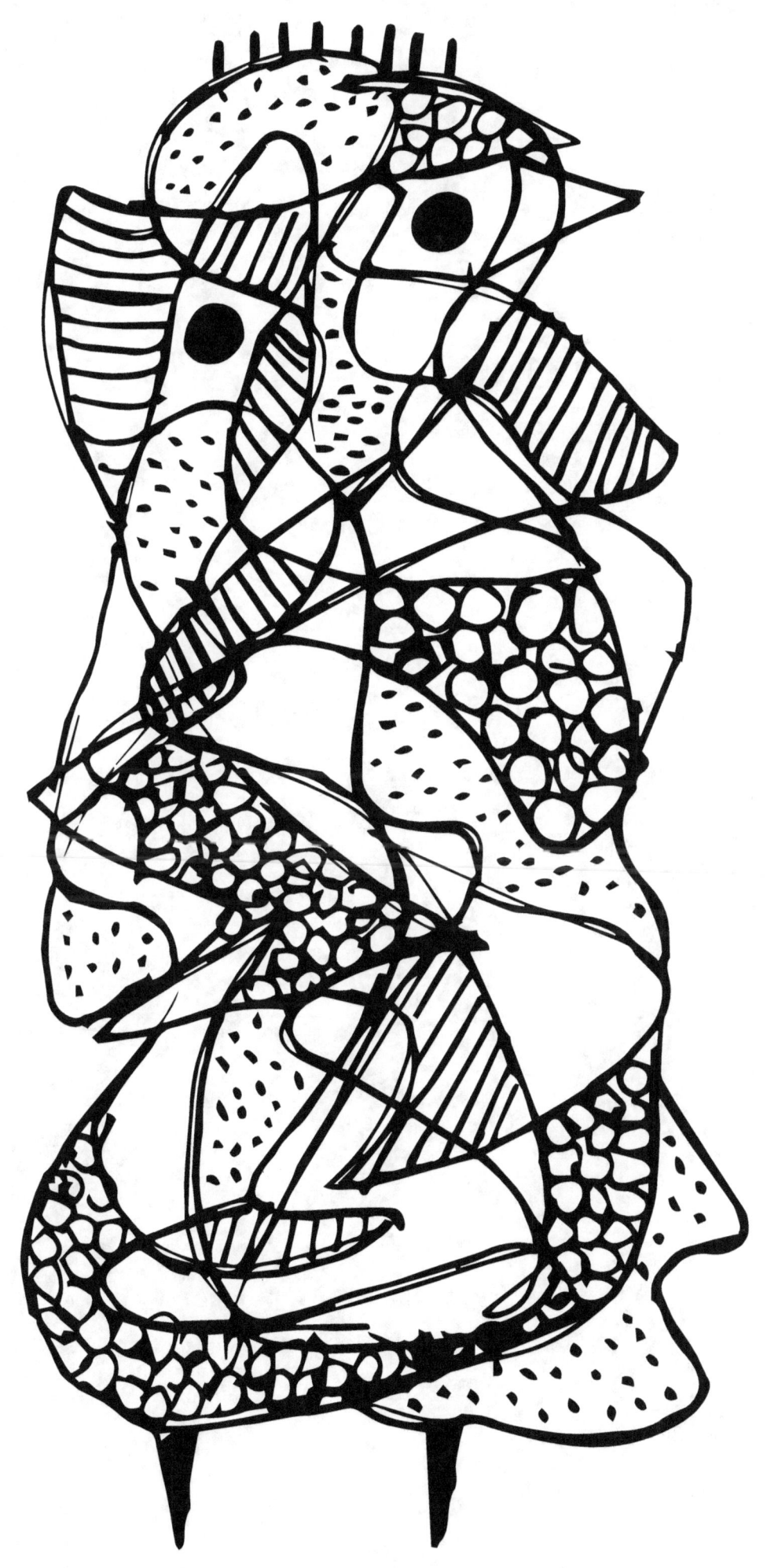

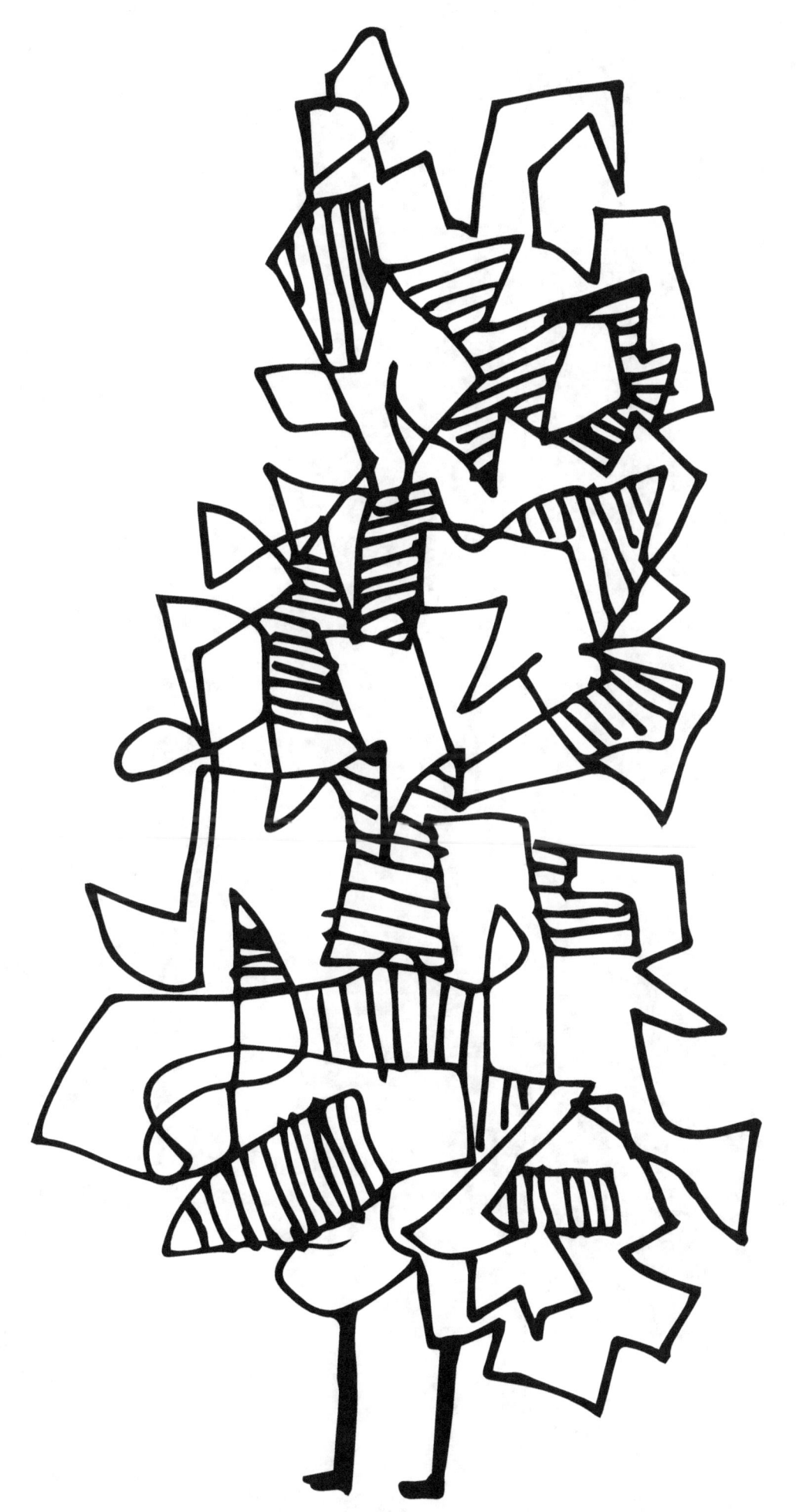

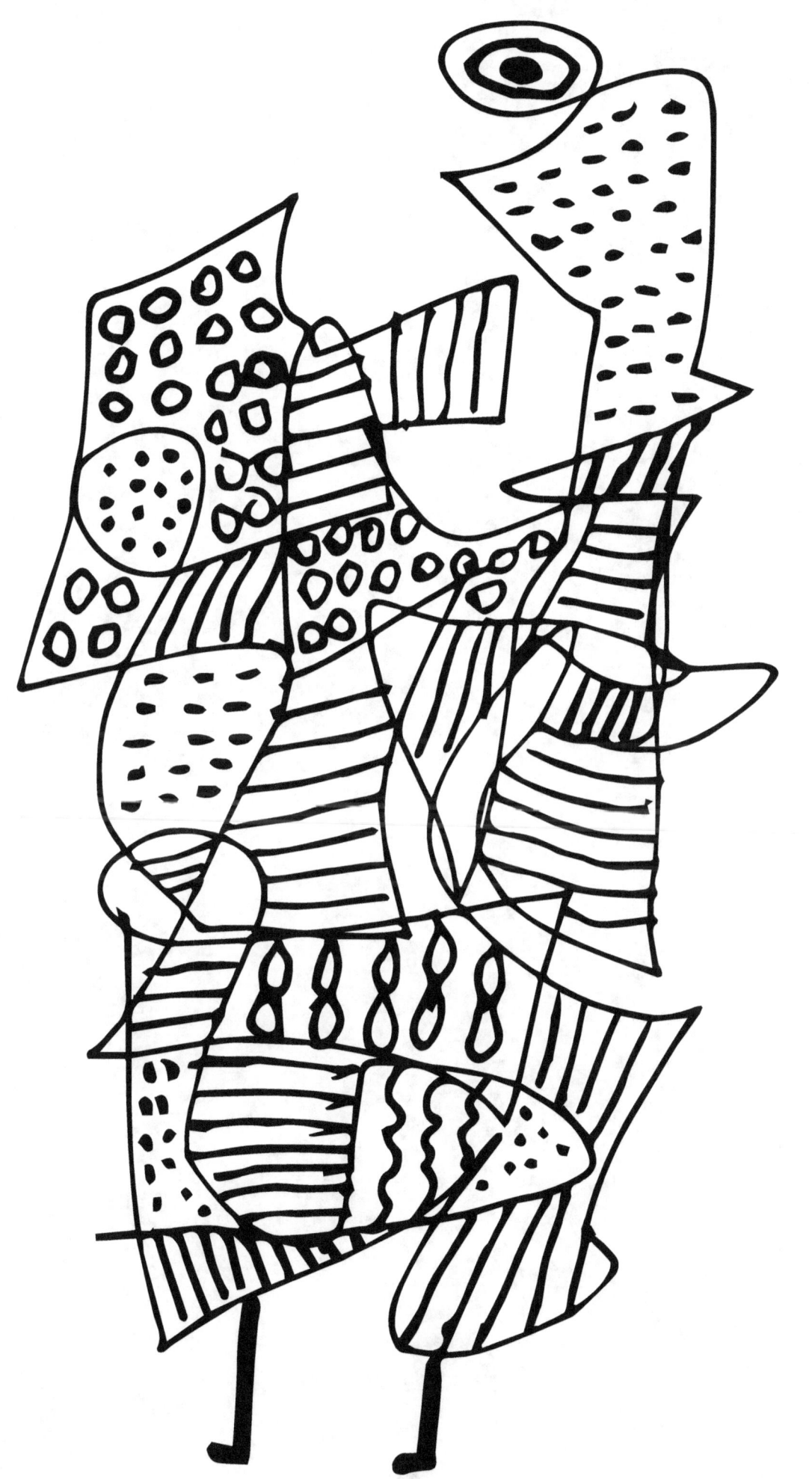

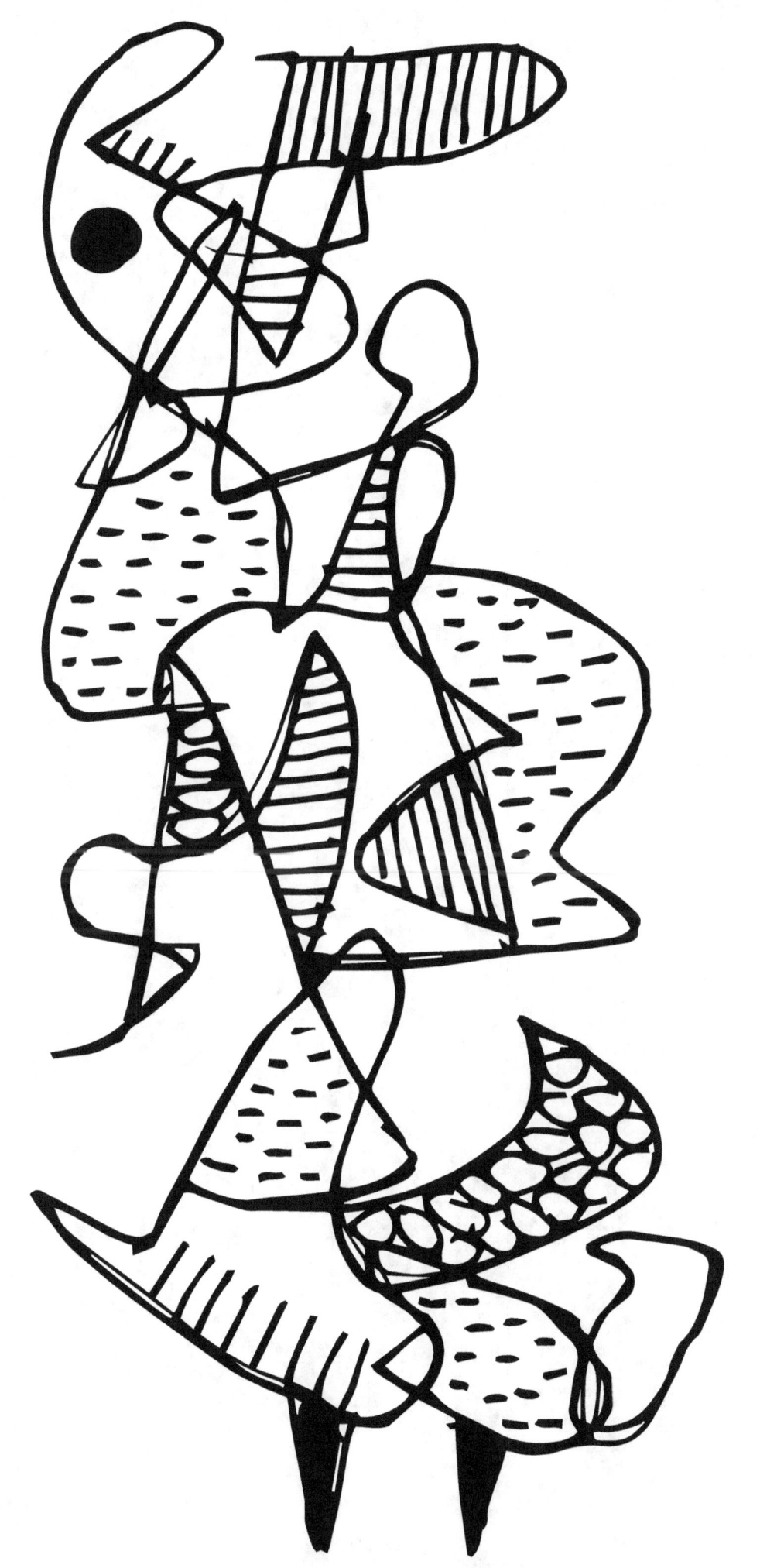

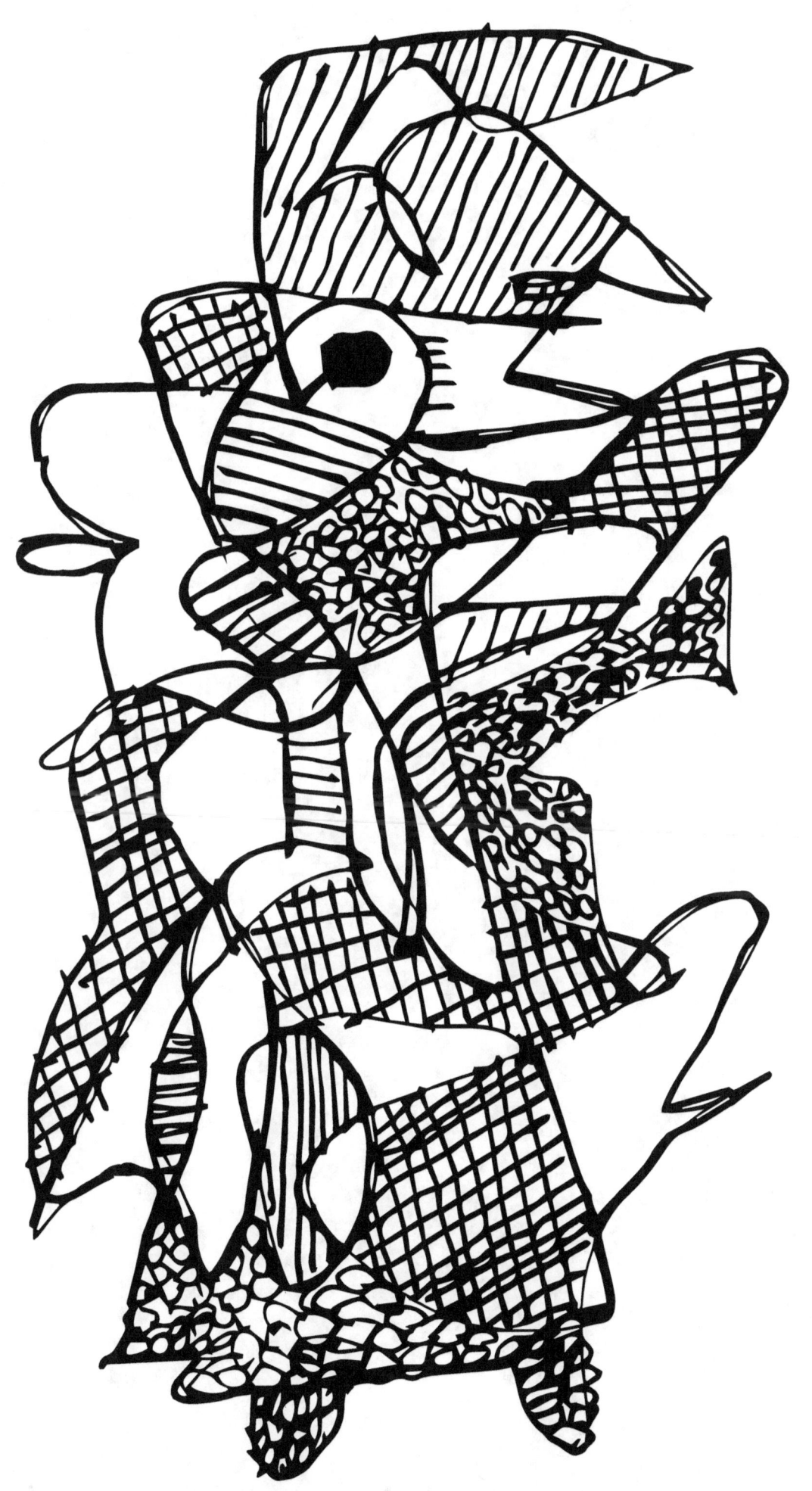

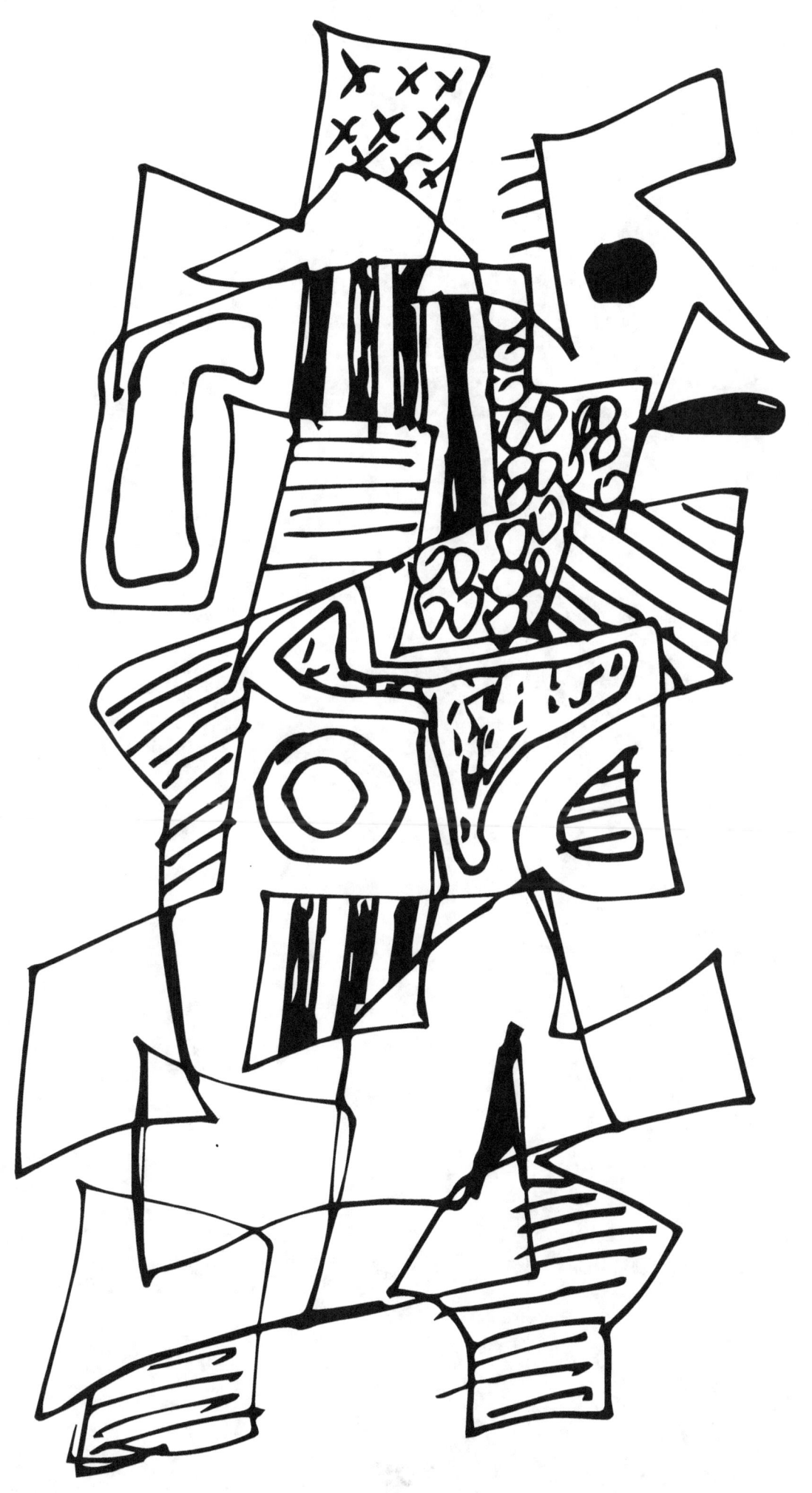

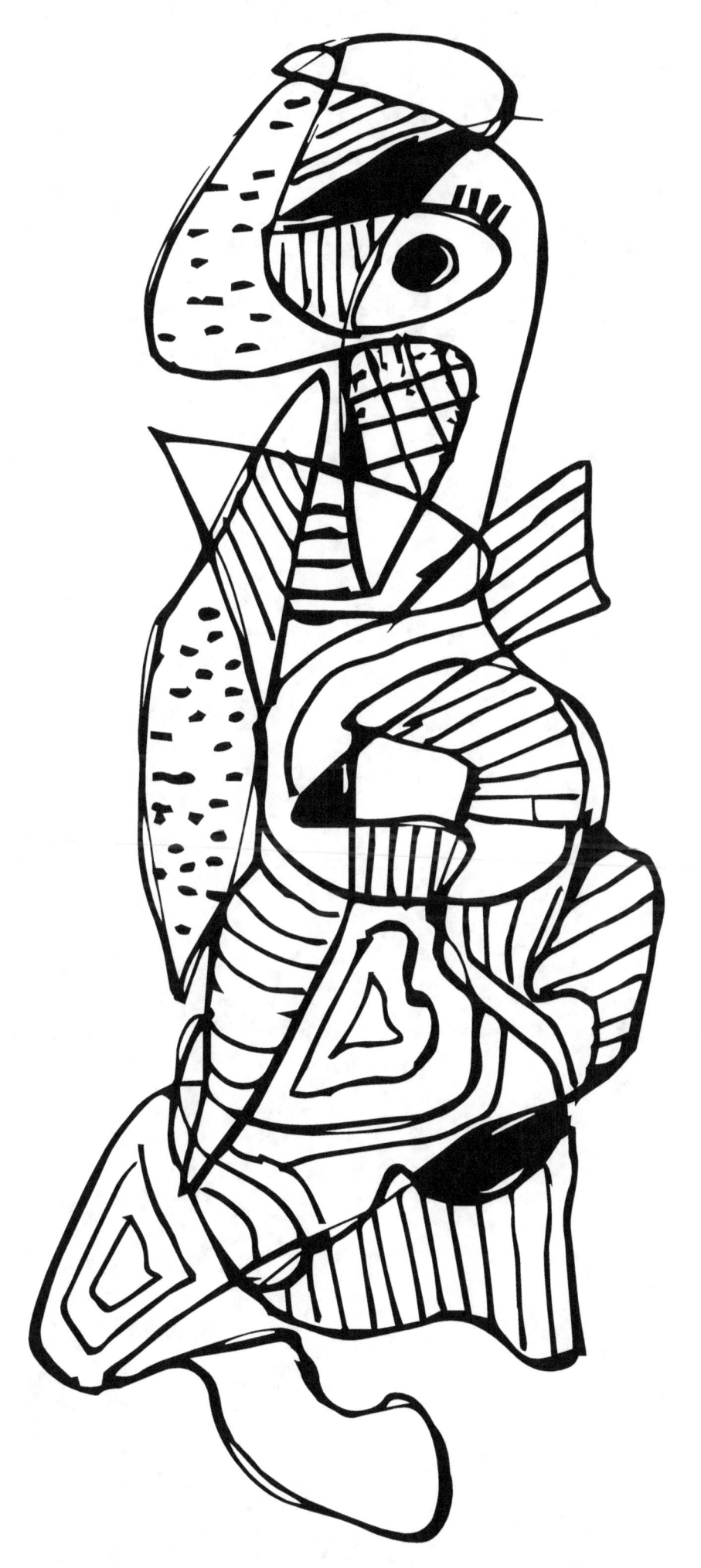

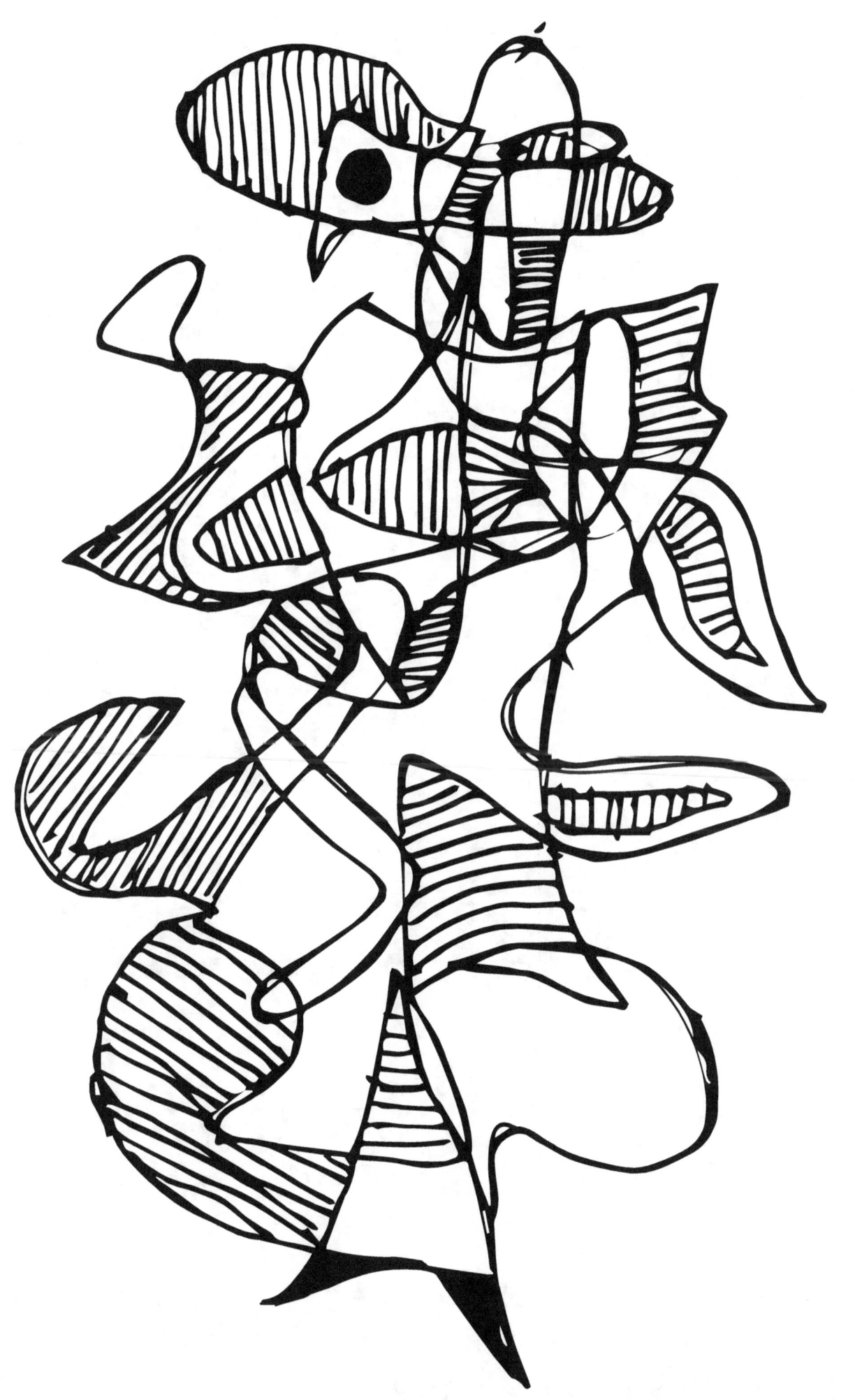

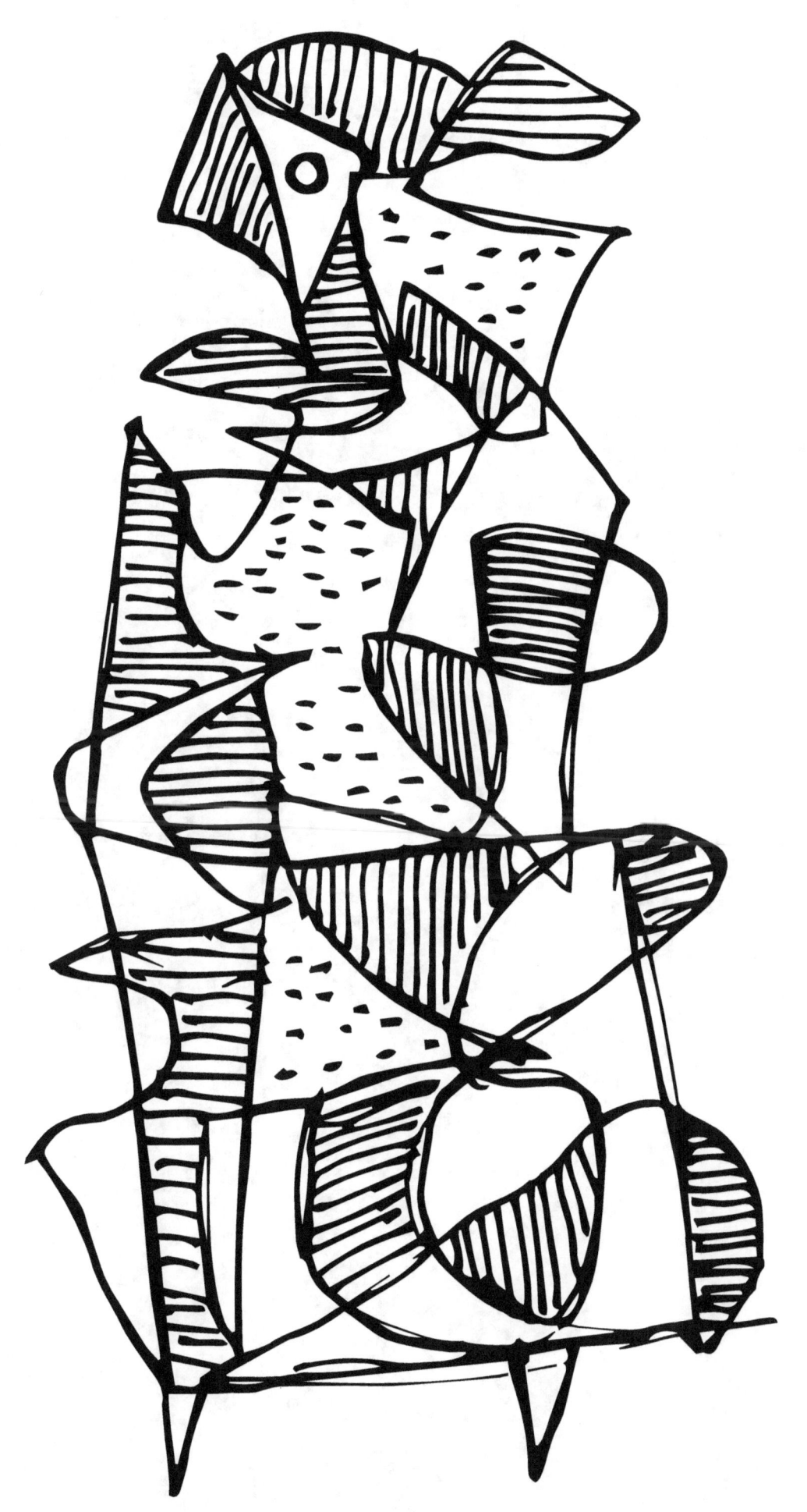

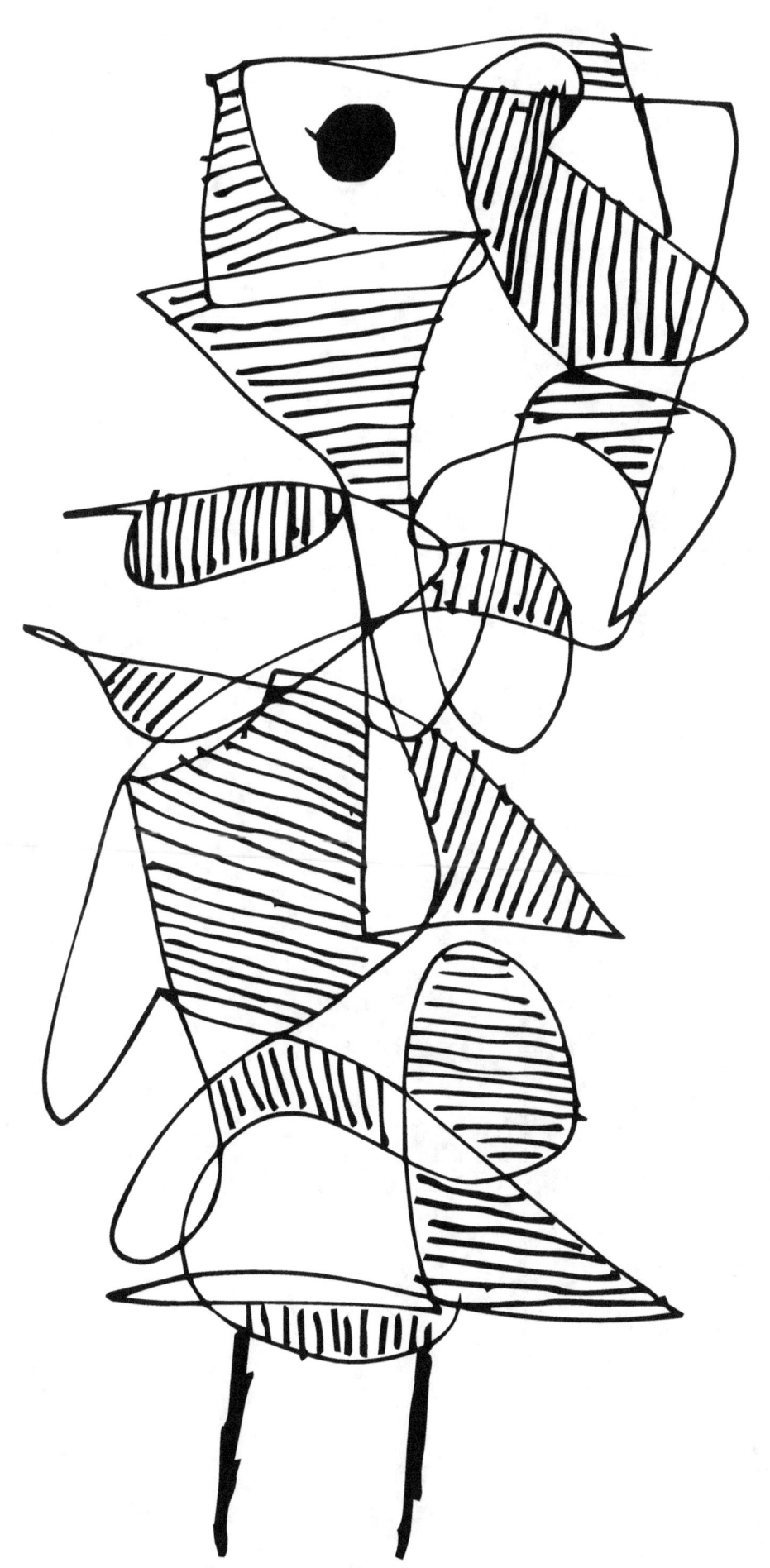

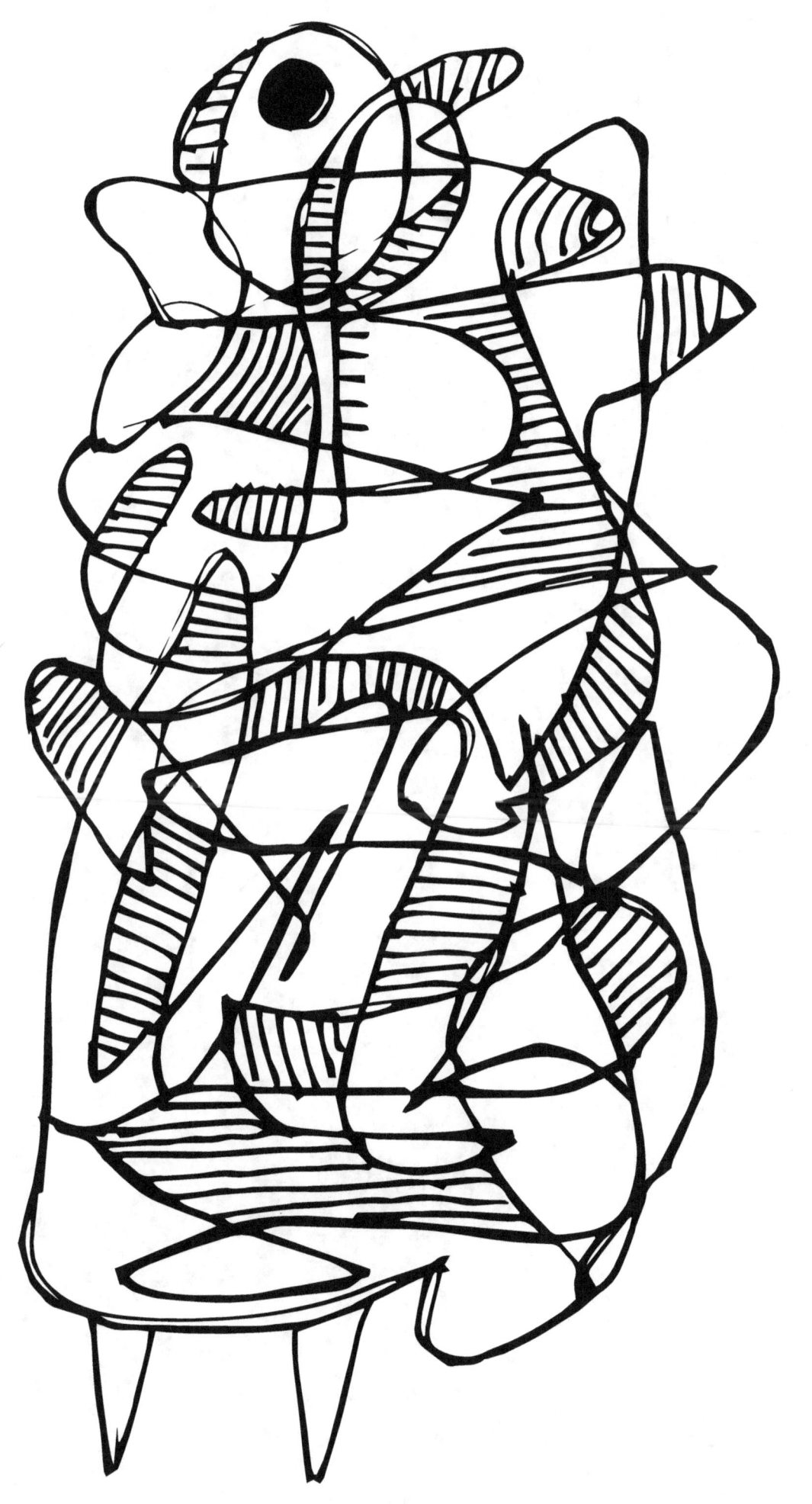

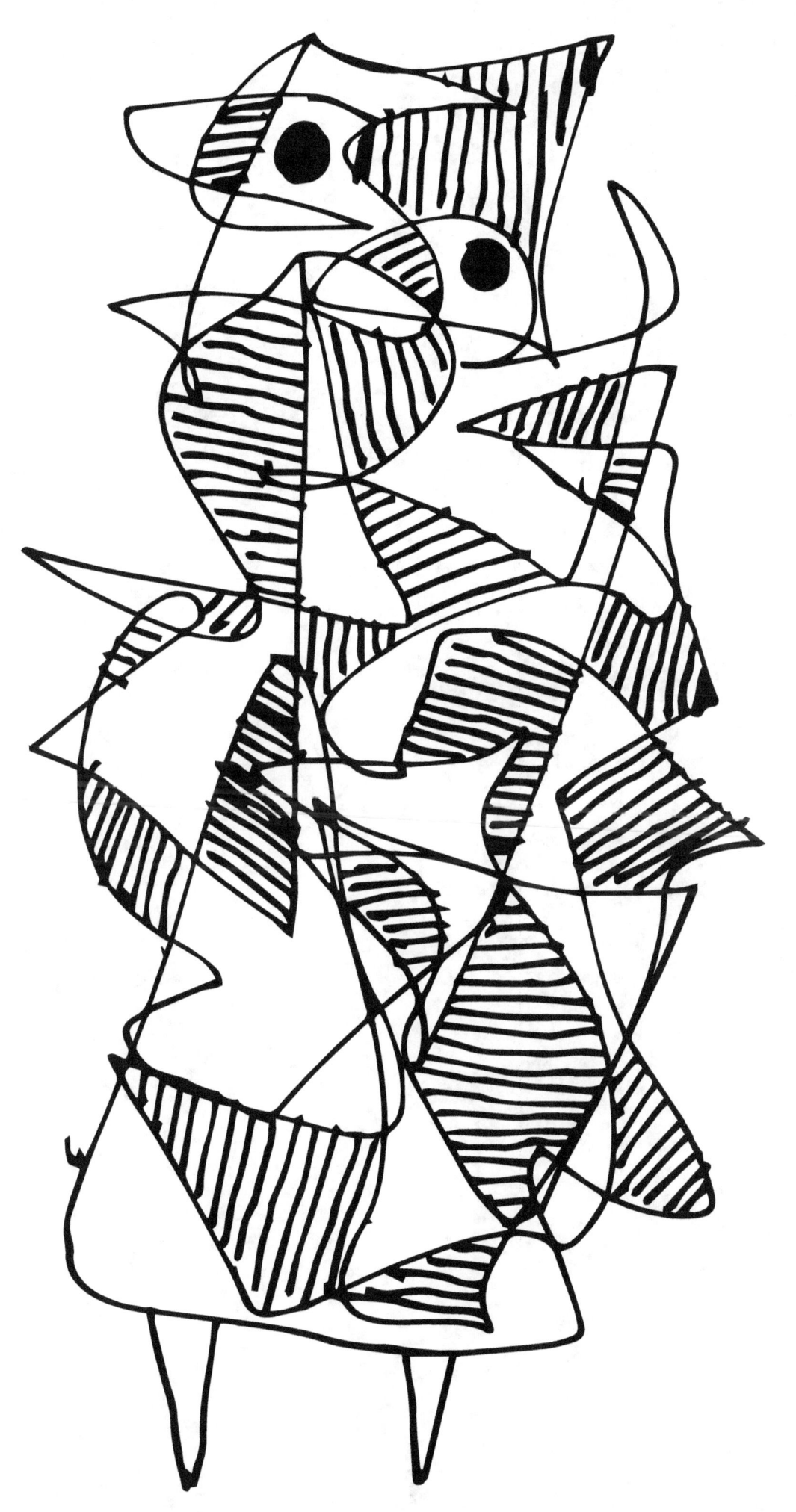

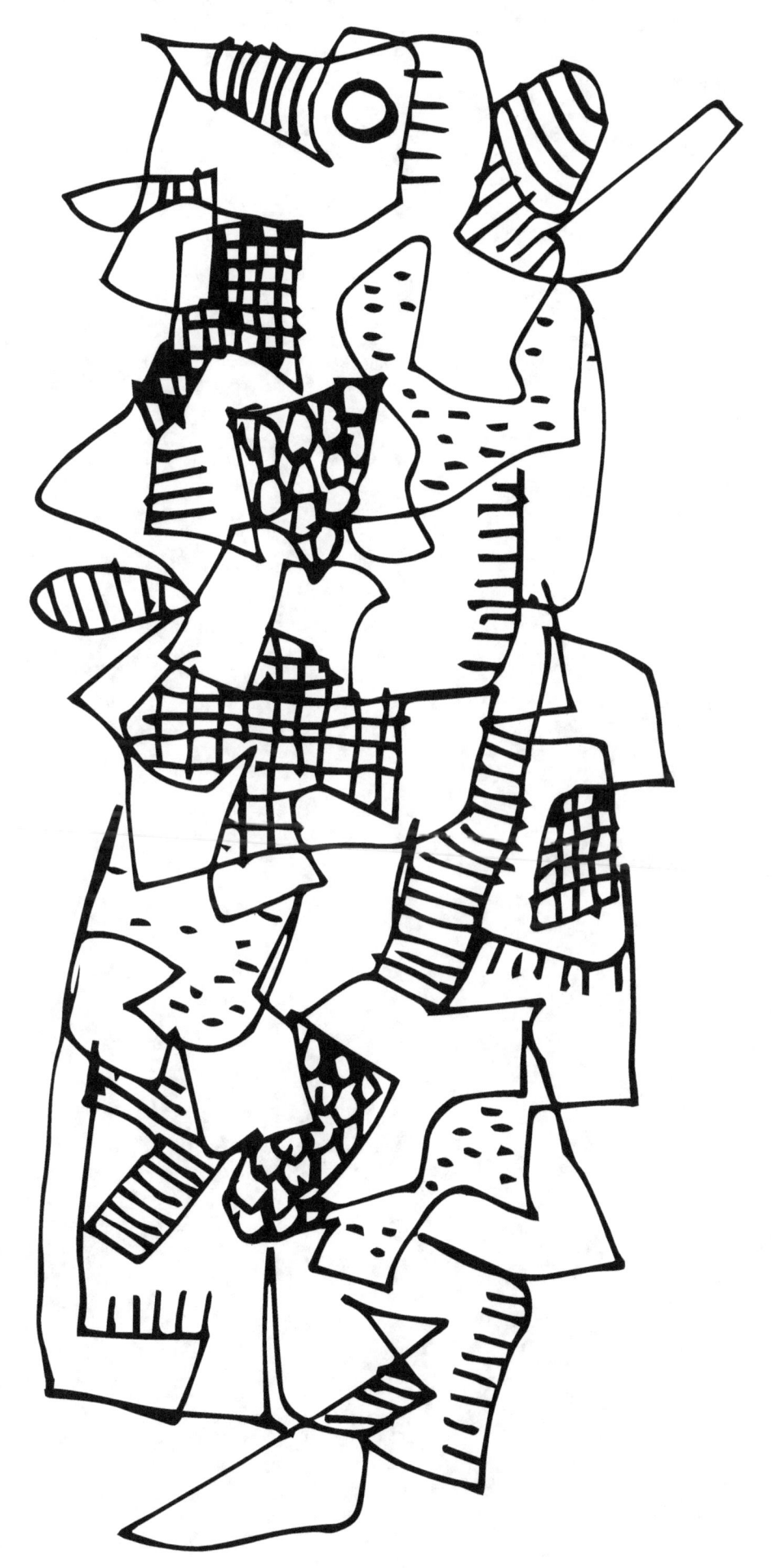

119

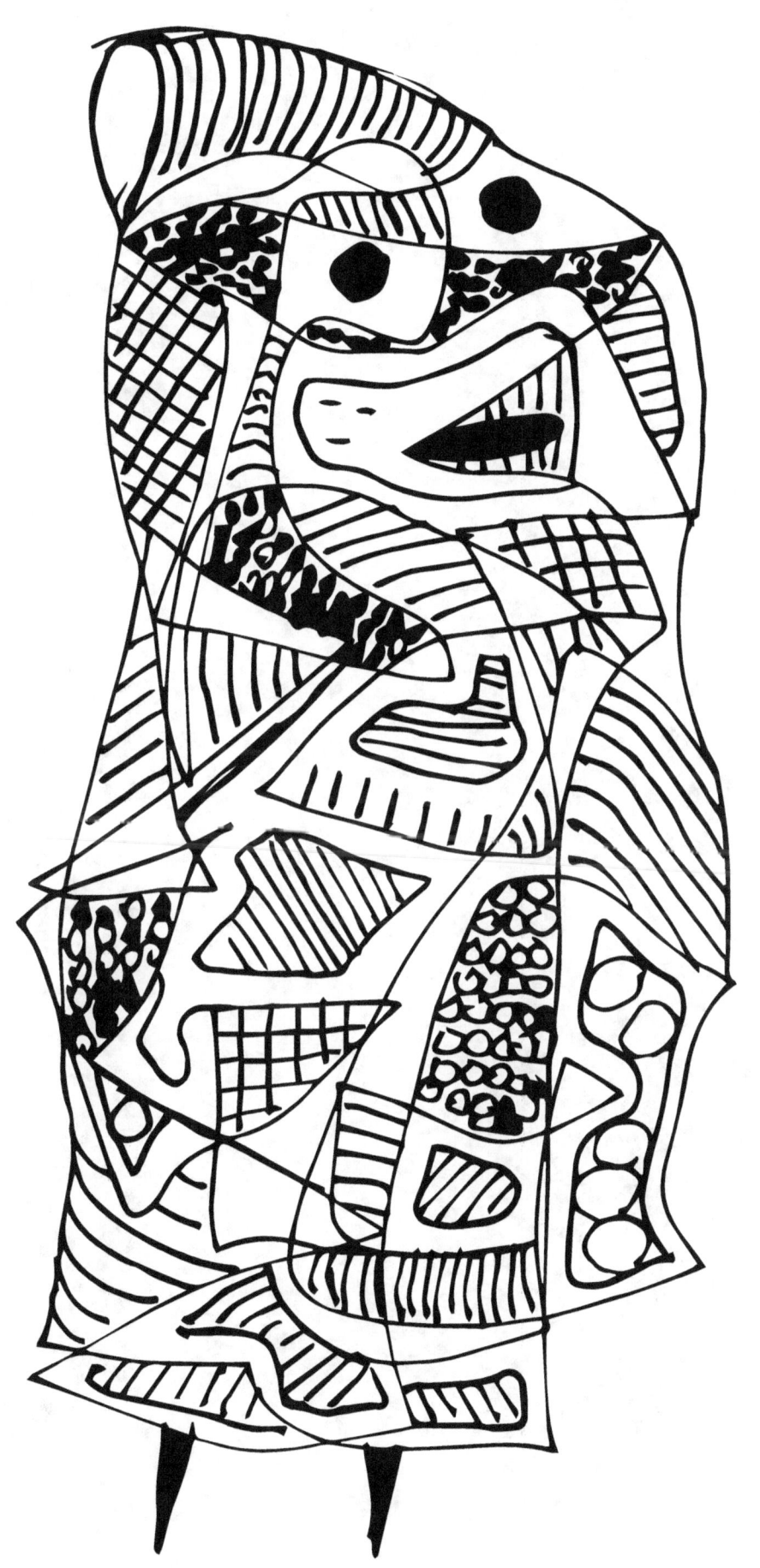

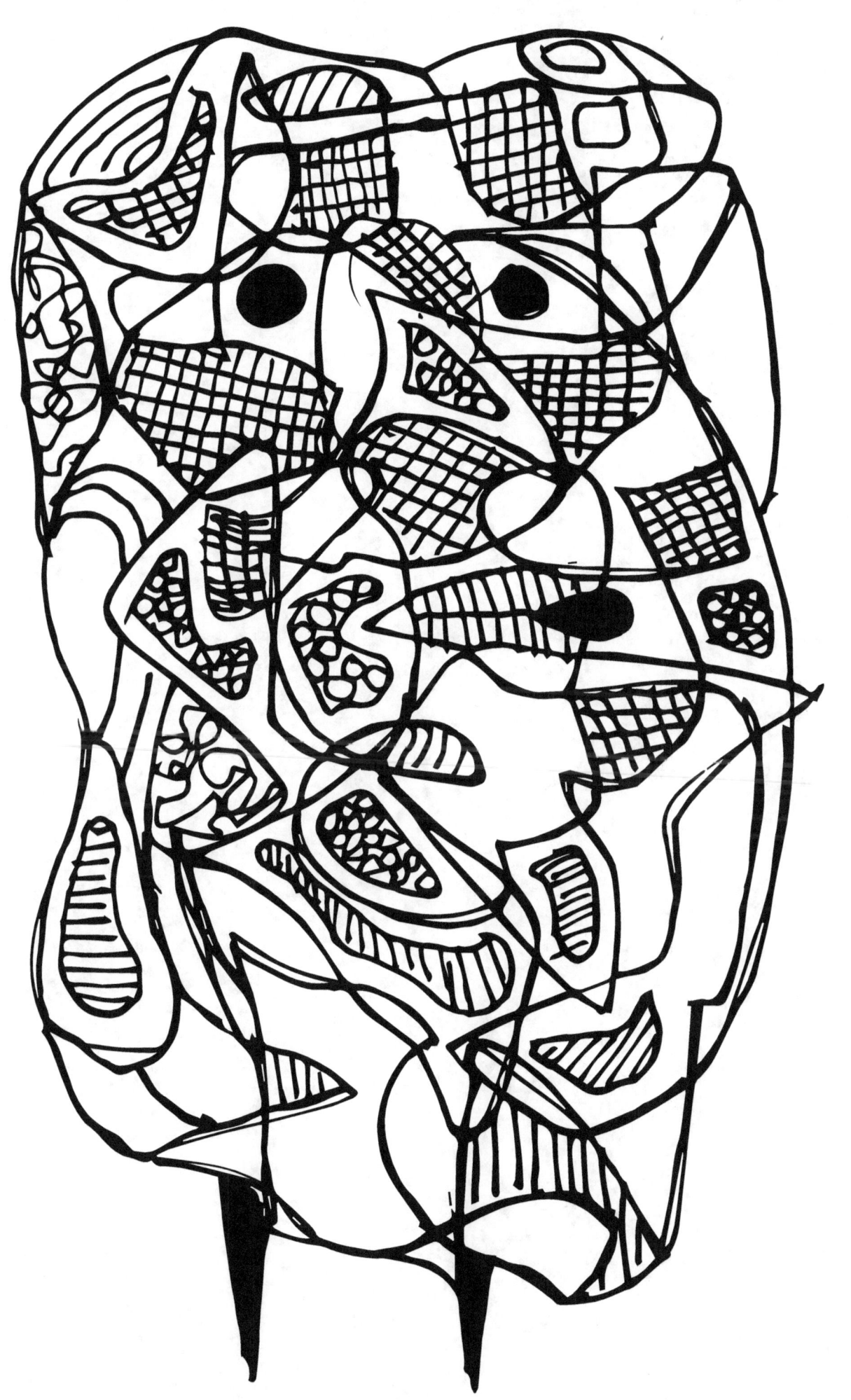

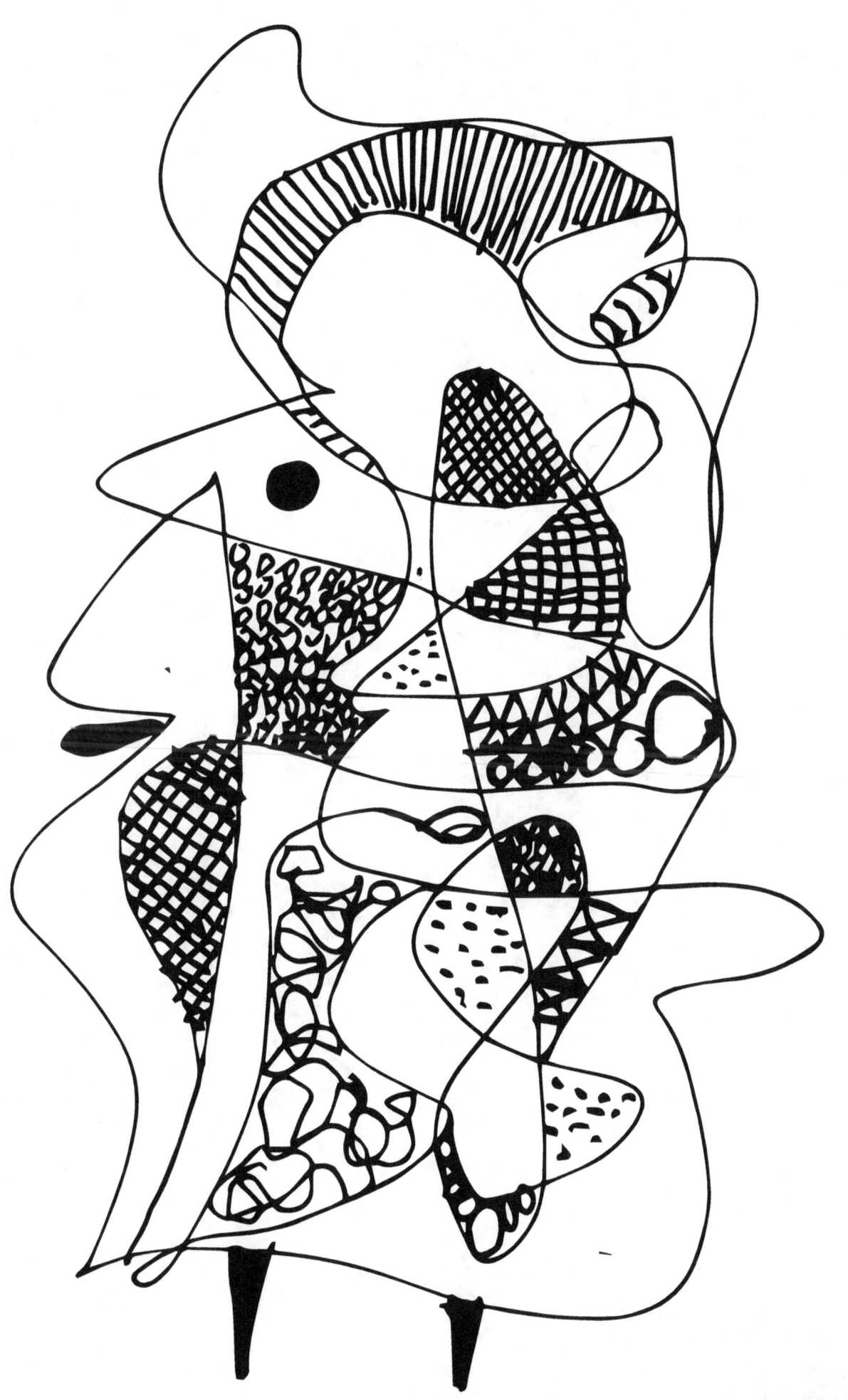